PELICAN BOOKS

ROMAN BRITAIN

Dr I. A. Richmond was educated at Ruthin School and Corpus Christi College, Oxford, and was a Craven Fellow and Goldsmith's Senior Student of the University, becoming a lecturer at Queen's University, Belfast. He later became professor of the Archaeology of the Roman Empire at Oxford University. He was also Director of the British School at Rome, where he wrote a standard work upon the Imperial City wall. He was Director of the Society of Antiquaries of London, a Vice-President of the British Academy, and a Royal Commissioner of Ancient Monuments in England and in Scotland. He excavated widely upon Hadrian's Wall and many other Romano–British military sites. He died in 1965.

THE PELICAN HISTORY OF ENGLAND

I. A. RICHMOND

ROMAN BRITAIN

PENGUIN BOOKS

Penguin Books Ltd, Harmondsworth, Middlesex, England
Penguin Books, 625 Madison Avenue, New York, New York 10022, U.S.A.
Penguin Books Australia Ltd, Ringwood, Victoria, Australia
Penguin Books Canada Ltd, 2801 John Street, Markham, Ontario, Canada L3R 1B4
Penguin Books (N.Z.) Ltd, 182–190 Wairau Road, Auckland 10, New Zealand

—

First published 1955
Reprinted 1958, 1960
Second edition 1963
Reprinted 1964, 1966, 1967, 1970, 1971, 1973, 1975,
1977, 1978, 1979, 1981

—

—

Made and printed in Great Britain by
Hunt Barnard Printing Ltd, Aylesbury
Set in Monotype Baskerville

CONTENTS

LIST OF ILLUSTRATIONS

LIST OF PLATES

LIST OF FIGURES

AUTHOR'S PREFACE

DURING this century the subject of Roman Britain has grown, and grown so large that all aspects of it cannot be covered in a small volume. Many aspects, moreover, are so technical as to demand more specialized treatment than is here appropriate. The choice of subject and treatment has therefore followed the author's own inclinations, dictated by the subjects upon which evidence rather than conjecture holds the field. For the use of those who would explore further a bibliography for each chapter is included, not in itself complete but sufficient to equip those who use it to the full to find the way about the subject for themselves.

I.A.R.

Oxford, 1963

CHAPTER ONE

MILITARY HISTORY

THE earliest political connexion of Rome with these islands came so suddenly that it was almost the first connexion of any kind between the Roman world and Britain. During the five years which preceded the invasion of Julius Caesar in 55 B.C. the Roman frontier had been advanced from the Alps and the Cevennes to the shores of the Channel: and, while there is evidence that in Gaul Roman merchants had for some time exploited the possibilities of trade in the areas then being occupied by Roman troops, there is no suggestion that they habitually crossed the sea to Britain. In contemporary literature knowledge of Britain is second-hand, derived ultimately from stray voyagers' accounts, garbled and misunderstood, or sometimes, as in the case of the best of all, disbelieved because the truth seemed stranger than fiction. Roman public opinion felt distant Britain as almost legendary, the source of mineral wealth, its very size and definition as an island in doubt, a new world of awesome isolation and uncharted risk. This explains the excitement with which Rome received the news of an invasion of Britain by Caesar and judged it an exploit of unexampled enterprise and daring, adding new laurels to him who had conceived it and new prestige to the name of Rome.

If this was the effect upon the Roman audience to which Caesar was playing, the effect at the scene of action was stunning. In two swift invasions in successive years Caesar had come and gone. Not scatheless; ignorance of the Channel tides twice took a heavy toll in ships, and

British chariot warfare proved disconcerting in its supple
mobility. But not unrewarded; Cassivellaunus, the principal dynast of the south-east, had offered unconditional
surrender; a powerful and friendly tribe, the Trinovantes
of Essex, had accepted Roman protection; hostages had
been given and taxes had been assigned. If the objective
of the expedition was, as Caesar alleged, to prevent
British powers from aiding the Gauls, then it might be
considered amply achieved. If annexation was intended,
the first steps had been taken, following which a definite
occupation might later be planned.

It is well known that events took a different turn:
Caesar's energies and ambition being diverted first by the
Gallic revolt and presently by civil war; while Augustus,
heir to his destiny but not to his temperament, cautiously
built up a new political system which required so much
consolidation as to encourage no cross-Channel venture.
This time it was the Britons who were the distant political
audience, and upon them the achievements of Augustus
and his successors were not lost. There was no doubt, for
Caesar had demonstrated this once and for all, that
Britain lay within the Roman grasp: and all kinds of
motives might set the military machine in motion: personal ambition, economic covetousness, or a political
grievance. The two former were outside British calcula-
tion, but the last could be studiously avoided, the more so
since Rome conveniently forgot to require Caesar's conditions of tribute. Meanwhile, there was the reality of the
Roman export and import market, now brought within a
fine day's view. This could provide a British chief with
luxuries of a kind unobtainable elsewhere and highly
appealing to an uninhibited sense of enjoyment, among
the foremost being the luxuries of the table and imported
wine. The new impulse given to trade is reflected by the

widespread adoption of coinage on the Gallic model throughout south-eastern Britain, in those denominations of silver and gold which go with commercial interest in luxury articles only.

But the proximity of Rome had another social effect, apart from the allurements of high life. Tribal society, as conceived in Celtic terms, was not a democracy or a tyranny but an oligarchy, which took the form of government sometimes by a council of nobles and elected magistrates and sometimes by a king and his counsellors. In such states the presence of strong factional interests was inevitable, and it was natural that such factions should endeavour to enlist the favour of sanction of Roman support, in reality or pretence. The reigning faction would be anxious to assert its position, the exiled rival always hopeful that Roman support might be brought, or bought, to redress the balance. This explains alike the Latin legends and Roman political forms on the coinage of reigning dynasts or the appearance of British kings as suppliants of Augustus or worshippers of Jupiter Capitolinus. But it need not imply that the policy of such rulers conformed to the sanction which it invoked. There is, on the contrary, every indication that, apart from correct external relations with the great power, British dynasts went their own way. The most striking case of actual reversal of Roman policy is provided by the fate of the Trinovantes, whom Caesar had specifically protected against their powerful and aggressive neighbours, the Catuvellauni, of Hertfordshire and district. This did not save them from complete absorption by the Catuvellauni some fifty years later, a step which advanced Cunobelinus, the contemporary representative of the line of Cassivellaunus, to virtual suzerainty of south-eastern Britain. His realm seems to have embraced the Chilterns and the

middle Thames valley, as well as Essex and part of Kent.
The Trinovantian lands, however, were the richest, and
it was there that Cunobelinus established, about A.D. 10,
his new capital of Camulodunum at Colchester. By
Mediterranean standards the place was not a town at
all. It covered a huge area, twelve square miles enclosed by
great dykes, but habitations were concentrated in small
scattered units. Mercantile and productive activity lay,
as might be expected, along the riverside, and excavation
shows that overseas trade was brisk. Here were concentrated the moneyers, whose moulds, for silver blanks
which were to be struck as coins, themselves strike the
imagination by their crude ingenuity. Like most ancient
rulers, Cunobelinus used his coinage for self-advertisement. It records the name of his new capital, Camulodunum, 'the fortress of Camulos', the war-god whom the
Catuvellauni had brought with them to Britain from the
plains of north-eastern France and who had hewn them
out a fair heritage. But the most constant type is the
lovely reverse with the corn-ear, reminding us not only
that this was the natural product of Essex acres but that
the contemporary geographer Strabo mentions corn as
one of the principal British exports. 'Corn, cattle, gold,
silver, and iron', runs his list: 'these are brought from
Britain; also hides, slaves, and clever hunting-dogs'.
Minerals are not found in the territory of Cunobelinus;
he must have drawn his silver from Derbyshire or
Somerset and his iron or gold from further west. But
the other items in the list could all have figured among the
exports of his kingdom, and we get a picture of how the
imports of such a Celtic prince were balanced. The subject Trinovantes would produce the corn, the middle
Thames and the Chilterns the cattle, the forests the hides
and pelts, the aristocratic kennels the hunting dogs. The

slaves form a darker picture, recalling the fact that no neighbours of a thriving native kingdom were exempt from slave-raiding and head-hunting, accepted respectively as the profit and proof of martial prowess. The imports were numerous. Wine, represented by the great containers of coarse pottery in the tombs of native noblemen; silver table-ware and bronze-plated furniture from the same sources; fine pottery from Italy and from southern and north-eastern Gaul, can be reckoned as tangible proof. Strabo mentions, in particular, ivory, jewellery, and glass. But there must have been much else of frailer constitution which has not survived. The tale is rounded off by two specially significant objects from the Essex area. Amid the burnt remains of a princely cremation at Lexden, near Colchester, was found a carefully mounted medallion of Augustus, which had been cast on to the pyre with other particularly valued possessions of the dead nobleman. The mounting is Roman, and the whole object is evidently a special present from the Roman world and of official import, precisely comparable with the portrait of King or Queen treasured by a paramount chief. No less remarkable is the little portrait bust of the Emperor Gaius (Caligula) from Colchester: nobody valued the memory of this mad and capricious ruler after his death, and the bust acquires meaning only as a contemporary token of regard by a philo-Roman notable at a time when Roman intervention was fully expected.

In other areas of the island changes which took place between the days of Caesar and Augustus were much less propitious. King Commius of the Gallic Atrebates, once the trusted emissary of Caesar to British kings, broke altogether with Rome after the great revolt of 53–52 B.C. and fled overseas to Britain. It may be presumed that he

and his followers were the principal figures in the tribe of
British Atrebates, and his descendants are later found
issuing coins spread over Surrey and Kent. The example
of flight from Caesar's wrath was followed by many, high
and low, from north-western Gaul, where the vengeful
hand of Caesar fell heaviest. For them the easiest land-
fall was the coast of Dorsetshire and Hampshire, long
open to cross-Channel commerce. They found there a
culture and people akin to their own, but here too the
newcomers brought new names. It is not clear that they
were responsible for the name Durotriges, applied to the
folk of Dorset; but they certainly gave the name Belgae
to the tribe centred in Wiltshire, borrowing for a single
unit formed of various immigrant communities the name
once famous in Gaul as that of a ferocious confederacy of
tribes, noted for their savagery and independence. Their
cultural equipment reflects their mixed origins, but they
found and developed an art of fortification already introduced to the area from their old homeland by way of the
south-west. This was the defence in depth, with massive
rampart, multiple ditch, and barbican gateways. These
fortifications, the strongest and most complex that Britain
had yet known, were needed to overawe subject popula-
tions and to defy potential rivals. In this respect the warrior chiefs must have resembled the Norman overlords of
a later age with their new-fashioned castles and their
retainers. What they lacked was the common overlord to
whom fealty was due.

Amid this strife and commotion, which meant a grim
fate for the conquered or dispossessed, it is not surprising
that few other stable communities emerge in south-
eastern Britain. For some time after the reign of Augustus
southern Surrey and Sussex appear to have been the
dominion of one Verica, of the lineage of Commius,

whose coinage displays the vine-leaf as its outstanding emblem. This ought to mean that, just as Cunobelinus extolled the wheat-ear as the basis of his commercial prosperity, so Verica owed much to the vine or its products. Verica, like both his elder brothers, Eppillus and Tincommius, uses on his coinage the title *rex*, which implies either Roman recognition or the desire for it: and that explains why, when he was driven out of his kingdom shortly before A.D. 43, he should have gone overseas to appeal to Rome. Verica's expulsion seems to represent the final and most successful drive of Cunobelinus and his sons towards the south. In the Thames valley the struggle had been in progress, with varied success, for a generation or more; and this rivalry also had brought about the appearance of British suppliant kings at the court of Augustus. If Roman poets sometimes indulged in prophetic visions of a conquest of Britain, the island chieftains already viewed the event as a sobering likelihood.

None of the kingdoms so far described lay further than fifty or sixty miles from the coast, and all were clustered about Britain's continental front. Behind them lay older-established tribes, whose aristocratic families may indeed have included younger adventurers from the world which we have been describing but whose peoples had no reason to welcome the aggressive warrior kingdoms established on their borders. Such were the Dumnonii of Cornwall and Devon, the Dobunni of Somerset and Gloucestershire, the Coritani of Leicestershire and Lincolnshire, and the Iceni of Norfolk. The Dumnonii, rich in mineral resources, had as yet developed no coinage, a sure indication of backward commercial development. The Coritani seem to have used at first the coinage of their more powerful neighbours. Only the Iceni and Dobunni coined in abundance, the former in conservative style, the latter finally under Belgic conquerors. Wealth there was, and artistic talent to serve it, as is shown by the lovely mirrors and chariot-furnishings or, in a lesser field, the decorated pottery: and Roman products reached the area also, if in a thinner stream. This sphere was rather less pervious to Roman influences; partly because its own civilization was set and firm, partly because relations with the coast-ward tribes through which such influences must pass were bad, and partly because the coastward tribes were themselves absorbing the market. When the time came, these districts were to be among the most Romanized in Britain: all but the Dobunni were cut off from the new civilization by hostility, greed, and lack of enterprise.

Beyond them again lay the mountain or forest tribes. In Wales, the Romans were to come to know two as for-midable enemies; the Silures of Monmouthshire and Glamorganshire, and the Ordovices of Powys. Covetous of their richer neighbours of the plain, these tribes had made contact with the kingdom of Cunobelinus, through the Dobunni by their mineral wealth. The third Welsh tribe, the Deceangli of Flintshire, also famous for minerals, were an easy prey to Roman aggression when the time came. The relations of the Coritani, of Shrop-shire and Cheshire, are less certain. Their hill-fortresses were systematically dismantled by Rome and their hill-country remained garrisoned, as if they were at first hostile and later restless. Next came the Brigantes, a very large but loosely knit tribe, covering most of the six northern counties: 'numerically the largest tribe in Britain,' writes Tacitus, but of unreliable political stabil-ity, as the Romans were later to learn to their cost. Finally, the Parisi of east Yorkshire complete the outer fringe. These folk, like the Catuvellauni of Hertfordshire, had come from the north-eastern plains of Gaul, bringing with them a rich civilization of magnificent war-chariots, armour, and accoutrements. Once established in east Yorkshire, the tribe had swarmed: and their rich and characteristic armour or weapons can be traced through west Yorkshire to Cumbria, Galloway, and even Northern Ireland. It is clear that the aristocratic culture of the whole north must owe much to these pushful and restless adventurers. Those who stayed in east Yorkshire were of more settled nature. Before the Claudian conquest they were already welcoming Roman and Trinovantian products to trading stations on the Humber.

Almost a century elapsed between the invasion of Caesar in 55 B.C. and the conquest of Britain by Claudius in A.D. 43. The contrast in the political situation was enormous. In Caesar's time only a corner of south-eastern Britain was within purview. The south-west was closed and hostile, the interior impenetrable to inquiry owing to its bitter hostility to the tribes of the south-east. Before the Claudian invasion, the *pied-à-terre* gained by Roman merchants had widened into a vast sphere of influence. Their products had reached the Humber, Trent, and Severn and their knowledge of lands and peoples beyond this must have been far less vague than Caesar's knowledge concerning southern Britain. When the Claudian invasion came the responsible staff was able to draw its intelligence from a much wider and better informed circle of traders and merchants than had been available a century earlier, and there were exiled dynasts whose political information must have been both precise and valuable.

It will be evident that in Britain itself the possibility of Roman intervention in the affairs of the island had long been expected before the immediate causes of the event came about. These were themselves various: as in many political events, no single cause can be regarded as exclusively operative. First, there was the expulsion by Cunobelinus of his son Adminius, who fled overseas and made an act of submission to the Emperor Gaius in A.D. 40. This appeal had coincided with the mounting of an expeditionary force by Gaius, which never got further than Boulogne, owing to other preoccupations. A year or two later came the death of Cunobelinus, the division of his kingdom between Togodumnus and Caratacus, and the encroachment upon the kingdom of Verica, who fled to Claudius. With the exiled princes had no doubt gone other notables, and it was then that the Britons, having claimed extradition of the exiles in vain, made the foolish mistake of creating disturbances on the Gallic coast. This is the meaning of the laconic phrase of Suetonius, '*tumultuantes Britannos ob non redditos transfugas*'.

The military problem set by the disorders on the Gallic coast now began to take shape. If Britain were not to be absorbed in the Empire and were left to become anti-Roman with impunity, then the creation of an Atlantic frontier would be a necessity. This was not in itself impossible, since it would have perhaps demanded no more men than went to garrison Britain. But it was fiscally less advantageous, since it threw the burden of an extra garrison on to an Empire no bigger than before: in other words, the costs of an army against Britain were not to be offset by the revenues of a conquered Britain. Again, it would disturb the balance built up between the army commanders of the Danube and the Rhine, by placing in north-western Europe forces which outweighed any others within striking distance of Italy and the centre of Empire. This ran counter to the delicate statecraft of Augustus, who owed his power to an equilibration of his chief army commands, each the sphere of a

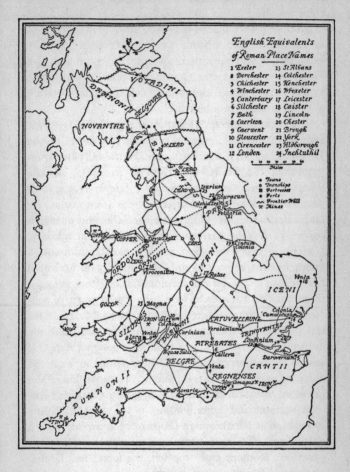

English Equivalents
of Roman Place Names

1 Exeter   13 St Albans
2 Dorchester   14 Colchester
3 Chichester   15 Kenchester
4 Winchester   16 Wroxeter
5 Canterbury   17 Leicester
6 Silchester   18 Caister
7 Bath   19 Lincoln
8 Caerleon   20 Chester
9 Caerwent   21 Brough
10 Gloucester   22 York
11 Cirencester   23 Aldborough
12 London   24 Inchtuthil

Figure 1

potential rival, and left the principle as a political legacy cherished by his successors. On the other hand, if the extra power were placed overseas, literally isolating it in an island-province, whence it could not return except by suborning a fleet subjected to a separate command, this measure would leave the Continental position very much as before and would thus solve both the fiscal question and the political problem at once.

The troops selected for the occupation were four legions, the Second Augusta, previously stationed on the Upper Rhine at Strasbourg, the Ninth Hispana from Pannonia, the Fourteenth Gemina from the Middle Rhine at Mainz, and the Twentieth Valeria Victrix from the Lower Rhine at Neuss. They were accompanied by many auxiliaries, including not a few Gallic and Thracian regiments. But the start was not auspicious. The soldiery, acutely disturbed by what seemed like banishment to another world, refused to embark, and only the arrival of a freedman as special commissioner from Rome brought them back to their duty in a tumultuous burst of self-respect. The time required for a report to Rome and for the dispatch of such a commissioner implies that the mutiny lasted not less than a month, and in one respect it served its authors well. The Britons, thinking that the outcome would be the postponement or abolition of the invasion, maintained no force to oppose the landing. Disembarkation and consolidation of a great maritime stores-base at Richborough (Rutupiae) were carried out unhindered. To save time and to distract resistance, which the Romans had expected, the forces had landed at three different points, presumed to be the natural harbours of Dover (Dubrae) and Lympne (Lemanae), as well as the main landing point on Thanet. Room for deployment was thus secured.

The Britons now rallied, depending as of old upon their tactical skill in chariot warfare. The leaders of the British forces were Togodumnus and Caratacus, but they depended too much upon natural obstacles and too little upon their power of manoeuvre, thoroughly underrating the ingenuity and resource of Roman troops in the face of river-crossings. At the first pitched battle, on the Medway, the Roman auxiliary troops crossed and caught the charioteers off their guard, and in the two-day battle which followed, Vespasian, commander of the Second Legion, achieved a successful surprise attack, while Hosidius Geta won a resounding victory by firmly sustained pressure and bold personal risk. The next river was the Thames itself, across which the Britons retreated without arranging for an effective rearguard action and allowed their retreat beyond the river to be cut off by Roman troops who had crossed uncontested, even using a bridge. The lack of counsel here displayed was no doubt due to the previous death of Togodumnus: and it is the more readily explicable when it is realized that, on the death of Cunobelinus, Togodumnus had taken the old kingdom, in Essex and Hertfordshire, while Caratacus had taken the kingdom of the middle and upper Thames, Hampshire, and Surrey. Thus, on defeat at the Medway, the Britons must in fact have split into two groups, one retreating westward under Caratacus, the other, leaderless, making headlong for home to north of the river. For nine long years Caratacus was to be a thorn in the side of the Roman army in Britain and was to gain many successes, some cheap and others dear: but history tells of his fighting only one more pitched battle, on ground of his own choice, when he risked all and lost all in a final and crushing defeat.

The way to Camulodunum lay wide open, but Aulus

Plautius, commander-in-chief of the expedition, chose now to halt at the Thames and to await the arrival of Claudius. The moment had come for which Claudius himself must have longed, when he could add a new province to the Empire, leading his army in triumph to the native capital and gaining thereby a success worthy of his long line of distinguished ancestors. The pride of the Claudian family was proverbial, but in this representative it was perhaps pardonable, for to him success in life had come so unexpectedly and so late. The ambition to add lustre to the Claudian name was certainly matched by a desire to obliterate from memory the nugatory performances of Gaius in this very theatre of war and so to uphold the reputation and glory of Rome. These motives too must certainly be taken into account in any assessment of the causes of the British war. Nor was the share of Claudius in the war wholly negligible. He himself took command of the advance beyond the Thames, fought a pitched battle with the natives, and then entered the royal city of Cunobelinus in triumph: and history records that other exploits, packed into a sixteen-day campaign, forced unnamed tribes into surrender. Two further scraps of information have come down to us. Other tribes were already voluntarily making their submission; and the Roman Senate, abrogating its constitutional right to ratify treaty terms, announced its willingness to accept, as valid, agreements concluded on the spot by Claudius or his legates.

Among the earliest of the native potentates to ask for a treaty was Cogidumnus, who inherited the kingdom of Verica, in Sussex. The value of his adhesion to the Romans was considerable, for it gave them a needed springboard for the next stage in the conquest, the attack upon the Durotriges and Belgae of Dorsetshire and Wilt-

shire. As a reward Cogidumnus in due course received
at least two other tribes as subjects, and the unique title of
rex et legatus Augusti in Britannia, marking him at once as a
native prince and a Roman official, whose sphere was
extra-territorial to the rest of the province. When he died,
the arrangement did not continue: but the memory of it
lived on in the name of his people, the Regnenses, or
people of the native kingdom (*regnum*). Another native
potentate, famed far and wide for his wealth, was quick
to secure it by rapid submission. This was Prasutagus,
king of the Iceni of Norfolk, whose friendship was also
welcome because it secured the right flank of the Roman
advance. But his subsequent record was less satisfactory
than that of Cogidumnus, whose reputation for loyalty
was of the highest. When the moment for disarmament
came, about four years later, Prasutagus did not carry all
his people with him and a large resistance group had to
be drastically repressed by Roman arms, for the movement was spreading to other tribes.

Meanwhile, Vespasian, whom fate was ultimately to
make Emperor, was occupied in mounting the offensive
against the west. It is unfortunate that for the account of
these operations we have to depend entirely upon secondary sources. No names are given, except that of the Isle
of Wight (Vectis), which was reduced to unconditional
surrender. The biographer of Vespasian speaks only of
two very strong tribes and the capitulation of over twenty
native fortresses (*oppida*). The two very strong tribes can
hardly be other than the Durotriges and Belgae, and, if
so, the fortresses lay in Dorset and Wiltshire. Two Dorset
hill-forts have furnished to archaeology dramatic evidence of their fate. The first, Maiden Castle, of which the
native name was Dunum (the fortress, *par excellence*), is
the biggest of all. In its final form, as seen today, it is still

vastly impressive. Two immense ditches form the outer
defences of two huge ramparts while the main entrance
is complicated by a double horn-work. The Romans had
these obstacles to face also: but they saw them crowned
with stockades and rendered sheer in stone and timber,
while the gates were blocked with massive doors and
overshadowed by great towers, as excavation has shown.
But excavation also revealed an emergency cemetery
within the hornworks, where the dead were hastily
interred during the Roman assault. The skeletons bear
evidence of the murderous effect of the Roman weapons.
The slashing cuts from the auxiliaries' swords, the stabs
from the legionaries' cut-and-thrust or the deadly little
square hole drilled in the skull by their throwing-spear
(*pilum*), the bolt from a field gun which stuck fast in a
spinal column: all attest the heavy fighting inexorably
pushed home which won for Vespasian his military
reputation. The anklets and toe-rings of the dead, on the
other hand, are the personal adornments of savages, the
manner of men who had to be faced. Discoveries of this
kind almost lift the veil of the centuries.

The second site is Hod Hill, north-east of Blandford, and
here the hand of Rome is self-evident. One corner of the
not irregular hill-fort which crowns a bold plateau is cut
off by the truly regular lines of a Roman fort, filled with
timber buildings of Claudian date and for some twenty
years the quarters of a legionary detachment and some
cavalry. What happened here is clear enough. While at
Maiden Castle, after surrender, a remnant of the inhabitants were allowed to use the dismantled fortress
and to live within its bounds, at Hod Hill the fortress,
slighted and emptied of inhabitants, received a garrison.
This marks a difference in treatment, and so it ultimately
worked out. In the neighbourhood of Maiden Castle, on

the site of the modern Dorchester, there was to grow up the modest Romanized capital of the Durotriges, amid a district full of well-to-do landowners. Hod Hill, on the other hand, is the south-western gateway to Cranborne Chase: and this remained a land of native farmers, consistently kept for generations at a uniformly low level of existence, like *fellahin*. Unconditional surrender here brought in its train not freedom but misery, and the legionary garrison was there to enforce its first organization, until the inmates of this special enclave had passed from subjects to serfs.

In the west the conquest of the Durotriges and the Belgae brought in new allies, or tribes in treaty relation. Foremost among these were the Dumnonii and the Dobunni. Both required Roman protection from their wilder neighbours in the Welsh hills and forests, and it is likely that the Second Legion garrisoned the south-west, perhaps at Exeter, while on the western fringe of their territory, at the Severn crossing of Gloucester (Glevum), a fortress for the Twentieth Legion was established in A.D. 49. Further up the Severn, at the gates of Central Wales, the Fourteenth Legion was established at Wroxeter. How matters stood further north-east is uncertain. The loyalty of communities bordering upon the Iceni was very soon found to be shaky, and it may therefore have been precaution rather than a demand for protection which induced the Roman high command to quarter among the Coritani the Ninth Legion at Lincoln. At this end of the frontier, screened by Severn and Trent, which was thus being almost automatically roughed out, the northward thrust secured or brought about an arrangement of great political importance. The very large canton of the Brigantes, which embraced the entire northern front, entered into treaty relations with Rome through their queen Cartimandua. The reason is not far to seek. During the next twenty years there were to be many proofs that this tribe in particular was prey to bitter partisan quarrels, in which its royal family took a leading part. The object of the alliance was thus to strengthen the queen's hand, and her action in A.D. 51, of delivering Caratacus into Roman hands after he had come within her grasp, shows her anxiety to insure with Rome rather than to honour a claim working against her inclinations. But for the moment the alliance was of immense value to Rome, since it guaranteed comparative quiet on the northern front, and might seem for the future to promise that Roman garrisons need never penetrate the grim and profitless uplands beyond the Humber. Above all, it gave opportunity to wrestle with the problems presented by Wales.

The earlier dealings of the Roman high command with Wales seem at this distance of time to have been marked by a failure to view the problem as a whole. So far as any policy can be detected, the Roman plan seems to have been to deal with the tribes piecemeal, facing each problem as it presented itself: a plan without finality, which tended too often to leave the initiative in enemy hands. Many of the early ventures, too, were doomed to frustration or disappointment. The campaign of Ostorius Scapula in A.D. 49 against the Deceangli of Flintshire was robbed of its intended results by a disturbance among the Brigantes, which called for Roman armed intervention. Indeed, the two events may well have been connected; for the effect of subduing the Deceangli would have been to drive a wedge in between the unconquered Britons of the west and the north, a threat perhaps resented by the anti-Roman party among the Brigantes. Nor were the strategical implications of the situation unappreciated in other quarters. The next offensive by Ostorius was against the Silures, with whom Caratacus had found a refuge and an ideal terrain for guerrilla warfare. The interpretation of the situation by Caratacus is clear from the action which he took. A British victory might enable him to keep the Roman forces out of Wales for longer: but a defeat might result in an immediate closing of the route of escape to the north. This explains why Caratacus moved his field of operations from the Silures to the Ordovices of Powys, and determined to put the issue to the test in a pitched battle, after which, if matters went ill, retreat to the north was still possible. The battle was a complete failure: despite the careful choice of very advantageous ground, the Britons were outmanoeuvred and outfought, ejected from their chosen positions and temporary fortifications by the superior discipline and equipment of the Roman troops. Caratacus escaped, but his family did not, and he himself made the fatal mistake of putting himself in the power of Queen Cartimandua of the Brigantes. The previous disciplinary measures and the present victory of Ostorius convinced the queen that duty and expediency coincided. Caratacus was trapped and delivered to the Romans in chains.

The Silures, however, continued to defy Roman attempts to penetrate their territory, cutting off auxiliary cohorts and harassing legionaries. For the time being they had to be contained and no attempt seems to have been made to penetrate the territory of the Ordovices either. Once again the Brigantian client kingdom required attention. Cartimandua and her consort, Venutius, began an armed quarrel, in which Venutius was able to summon powerful external help. To restore order and induce a reconciliation Roman intervention with both auxiliaries and legionaries was required, without by any means immediate success. The shape of things to

come was now beginning to emerge. The Trent–Severn
frontier was not to provide the answer to the British
political problem: instability among the Brigantes and
downright hostility in Wales would demand the annexation and policing of much wider areas.

The next military operation on the Welsh front was one
of singular interest. The governor of A.D. 59, Suetonius
Paulinus, was a seasoned campaigner in Africa, where his
chief exploit had been to defeat the tribes of the Atlas
mountains by striking at the more distant plainlands
from which they were fed and reinforced. In mountainous
Wales, resistance was similarly nourished from the isle of
Anglesey, populous, hospitable to refugees, and the seat
of a large community of Druids, fanatically antagonistic
to Rome. The recent discovery of a great hoard of objects,
either devoted or destroyed but in any case certainly
belonging to the priestly community, has shown how far
their connexions ranged. The objects may have come as
offerings or as tithes of booty – they are all war material,
including the chains of captives: but they represent the
spoils or riches of districts extending from south-west
Britain to Yorkshire and even to Northern Ireland, represented by war-trumpets. Tacitus is so preoccupied with
the dramatic contrasts of the situation that he does not
quite clearly evaluate the connexion between the Druids
and the political side of the picture. In fact, it becomes
clear that Paulinus was not only wiping up a focus of
material resistance but wiping out a native cult of which
the influence was much more pervasive than any ancient
author hints. It was one of the rare native cults with
which the Roman government would make no com-
promise; not so much because of its tenets, which were
not devoid of interest to educated Romans, as because of
its use of human victims for augury and sacrifice. The

expedition was carefully prepared, with landing-craft
suited to the shallows of the Menai Strait, and the result
was decisive. Just for a moment the attacking legionaries
and auxiliaries, to whom magic and spells were a vivid
everyday reality, stood appalled at the sight of the
defenders, backed by praying and cursing priests and
accompanied by wild women devotees who ran amok
with flaming torches. Faith and discipline then triumphed
and the Roman battle-line pressed forward to victory.
The island was garrisoned and the sacred groves systematically felled. Copying the African campaigning,
Paulinus should next have undertaken the reduction of
the tribes whose source of supplies, propaganda, and
encouragement was now extinguished. He was prevented
from doing so by an unexpected rebellion.

During the winter of A.D. 59–60, or a little before it,
King Prasutagus of the Iceni had died. As a Roman
client-king, he could not legally bequeath the succession
to anyone, but his renowned wealth he had divided, giving half to the Emperor and a quarter each to his two
daughters. His widow, Boudicca, does not appear to have
been a legatee. In the absence of a male claimant to the
throne, the Romans did not nominate a client-queen,
Cartimandua having already proved a liability rather
than an asset: and, before absorbing the kingdom into
the province, began to divide the legacy, at the hands of
army officers and Treasury agents. A first step was a consolidation of Imperial property, which involved the
revocation of grants made by Claudius to tribal notables.
The relatives of the royal family were also made guaran-
tors for payments. The entire tribal aristocracy was thus
alienated by being treated as newly-conquered subjects,
culminating in the scourging of Boudicca and the viola-
tion of her daughters. The result was a wholesale revolt,

and this spread to the neighbouring tribe of the Trinovantes.

The Trinovantian rebellion had a rather different
cause. It is clear that this territory had been from the first
treated as conquered soil, whose inhabitants were at the
mercy and unconditional disposal of Roman conquerors.
On the site of the old native capital at Camulodunum, in
A.D. 49–50, the Romans began to lay out a new provincial capital, peopling it with a strong body of army
veterans. This meant the perpetual confiscation not
merely of land for the town but also of a sizeable land-
holding for each veteran, the size relating to army rank
previously held. Nor was captive territory assured of legal
protection from still further land-grabbing by Roman
settlers once established. The establishment of a strong
nucleus of veteran settlers in order to provide a focus of
loyal citizens as an insurance against possible rebellions
was not the sole purpose of the new *colonia*, as such a
foundation was called. The new capital was to be a focus
of provincial loyalty to Rome, which expressed itself, in
the fashion of the age, in an Imperial cult dedicated to
the living Emperor Claudius. The cult was to be served
by a high priest and priestess chosen annually from the
native allied and subject tribes from among their aristocracy and its duties involved not only the observance of
a calendared series of rites but the payment for attendant
festivities, shows, games, and musical or literary contests.
The expenditure involved might suit and even repay the
ambitious philo-Roman: others would grudge or resent
it, according as it hurt their sentiments or their pockets.
From the Roman point of view, it was the best method of
creating a united feeling of loyalty and of sublimating
tribal ambitions and rivalries, just as it was an admirable
means of inculcating Roman ideals and culture. It had,

moreover, succeeded well in Gaul, where, however, it took the place of an existing annual gathering and was spread over a number of communities six times as large. On the Trinovantes these burdens fell particularly heavily. Part of the tribe, presumably the people of Togodumnus and his estates, was being summarily ejected to make way for the *colonia* and its lands: part was attributed to the *colonia* for administration and a graded citizenship, and upon this would fall the burdens of priesthood and the like. Of the common folk, many were toiling in labour-gangs upon the building of the *colonia*, while others tilled the new estates for exacting ex-army veterans. It cannot be supposed that these victorious soldiers were the best representatives of Roman civilization: indeed, Tacitus does not mince words in describing their insulting arrogance and they have themselves left behind them a magnificent centurion's tombstone and some highly piquant caricatures in clay to remind us that in their own circles pomp and vanity were not unaccompanied by satirical insight.

The acts which aroused satire in the conquerors engendered bitter rage and humiliation in the conquered, and these in turn bred revolt. It is not surprising that the Trinovantes were ready to join the Iceni, and there were others whose adherence was secret and did not emerge in the form of communal action. The course of the revolt itself is clear. The first move of the rebels was against Camulodunum, where the building programme had concentrated upon the Temple of Claudius and a senate house and theatre rather than upon the fortifications which were to enclose them. All resistance was over in two days and the captives were butchered with merciless and inhuman cruelty, particularly those reserved for sacrifice in the sacred groves. The Ninth Legion, too late

to save the *colonia*, was itself very severely handled: two
thousand men were afterwards required to bring it up to
strength, and only the cavalry succeeded in escaping.
This failure allowed the revolt to spread. Paulinus himself reached London in time to take stock of the situation,
but his main body of troops was far behind and he did
not dare risk being trapped. He therefore regretfully but
firmly abandoned both London and Verulamium, which
soon perished in fire and slaughter behind him, and sought
to concentrate his troops before dealing with the enemy.
Word was sent south-westwards to the Second Legion
to join him and this implies that a concentration was
planned somewhere near the junction of the Fosse Way
and Watling Street, the two lines of communication
necessary to such a plan of action. But his hand was
forced. The Second Legion failed to move because its
acting-commander disobeyed orders: commissariat diffi-
culties were also acute in the late spring or early summer.
In the end Paulinus felt he could wait no longer, and
chose a battle-ground which gave him the maximum
advantage in the face of a developing attack. The Romans,
barely ten thousand strong, with a mixed force comprising one legion, a detachment, and auxiliary infantry and
cavalry, were gravely outnumbered. Even the British
casualties were later estimated at about eight times the
whole Roman strength. But the Britons were badly
equipped and armed, undisciplined and untrained,
dangerous perhaps only upon ground of their own choosing or in surprise attack: and their mood was over-
confident – they had even brought with them their
families in wagons to witness the expected victory. The
Romans had now chosen the battle-ground, on terrain
entirely favourable to their disciplined and deliberate
manoeuvre with greatly superior arms and armour. The

Roman wedge-formations, applied simultaneously at various points, with lancer-charges to break any nucleated resistance, threw the Britons into disorder and pinned them in a helpless mass against the wagon-lines with which they had blocked their own retreat. The battle degenerated into grim and pertinacious slaughter, in which the rebels paid in full for their atrocities, accomplished and intended. Boudicca fled, quickly to die either by taking poison or through illness, according to different accounts, and the Romans began a systematic wasting by fire and sword of rebels and waverers. In their plight the Britons had one powerful advocate on the winning side. The new procurator, or chief Treasury official, who could report independently to the Emperor, advocated milder treatment as a means to end resistance and censured Paulinus for the circumstances which had led to rebellion. No doubt he anticipated a severe shrinkage in revenue following the devastations: and his own department had been so shamefully to blame for corruption and mismanagement that it may have been well to direct attention elsewhere. But other factors must also be taken into account. The procurator was himself a provincial or North Italian, and had married the daughter of a Gallic aristocrat who had taken a leading part in implementing a liberal policy of the Roman government towards his own tribe after just such a revolt. Roman history presents no more illuminating example of the interaction of Roman and provincial feeling in the new world which was being created in Western Europe. The government took the hint, but handled the situation tactfully. A special commissioner was sent out to observe conditions and reported less severely. Suetonius, who deserved well for his handling of the crisis, whatever his attitude to the subjugated, was soon recalled and the province settled down to lick its sores under a milder governor. Only seven years were to elapse before civil war shook the entire Roman world, and imposed upon the victor the task of impressing the frontier lands with renewed proof of Roman vitality and power.

The Flavian dynasty was fortunate in its earlier governors of Britain. The first, Petilius Cerealis, who had been through the Boudiccan revolt as legate of the Ninth Legion, was a clear-headed and stalwart upholder of Roman liberal policy and a firm if trenchant general. The second, Iulius Frontinus, was a passionate believer in efficiency as the basis of the senatorial partnership in Imperial rule. The third, Iulius Agricola, new to the senate, invites criticism owing to the idealization bestowed upon him by his famous son-in-law, the historian Tacitus; but his shrewd competence and political common sense is not obscured by the theme of dutiful senator and ogre-Emperor. The work of all three governors hangs together, for it is the rounding-off of the British frontier problem.

The logical order of conquest imposed by the geographical formation of Britain requires that the subjection of the north should be preceded by the conquest of Wales. In A.D. 71, however, political events determined that this order should be reversed. Until then, the main theatre of war had been the Welsh border. But amid the world-wide uncertainty caused by the civil war of A.D. 69–70 northern Britain became the scene of a breakdown in Roman frontier policy which called for immediate attention as soon as the central government was strong enough to authorize it. The new situation was due to the collapse of the Brigantian client-kingdom as an organized philo-Roman community.

Failing the central portion of the *Annals* of Tacitus, history is silent as to the circumstances in which the

Brigantian realm had become a Roman client state. But the event had happened early, soon enough for Cartimandua the queen to demonstrate her loyalty by the extradition of Caratacus, in A.D. 51. Nor must it be forgotten that such an act of faith was needed: the Brigantes had already given trouble a year or two before, when Ostorius had attempted to cut the connexion between Wales and the north by absorbing the Deceangli of Flintshire. The diversion thus created had checked the Roman effort and had demanded direct interference, followed by executions and a general pardon, in Brigantia. Thrones of client-rulers had been declared vacant for less than this, and Cartimandua, in particular, had reason to lean upon Rome for support. When later organized as a Roman canton the Brigantes, numerically the biggest tribe in Britain, covered north and west Yorkshire, together with Lancashire, Westmorland, Cumberland, and County Durham. They may even have spread beyond the Solway, where the tribal boundaries are obscure. This great area, sundered by the Pennines and their spurs into numerous divisions, each large enough to maintain powerful war-bands, must always have owed its cohesion to mutual advantage and to local balances rather than to inflexible domination from a single centre: in other terms, Brigantian central power was an overlordship, embracing numerous powerful septs, rather than a direct and immediate autocracy. The ancient way of reinforcing such a suzerainty was by marriage alliances, and that is the characteristic which Tacitus emphasizes in his thumb-nail sketch of Cartimandua, declaring that she owed her power to aristocratic connexions. And when, not long before A.D. 57, Cartimandua quarrelled with her consort Venutius, her first move was to capture his relatives. The answer was the organization by Venutius of an invasion from outside the canton, thus demonstrating for the first time known to us the potential weakness of the kingdom and its liability to disruption. Powerful Roman forces were required in order to restore order. But the followers of Venutius were not themselves free from inconstancy. It was his armour-bearer, in Celtic society normally the son of a powerful vassal, whom Cartimandua presently espoused, doubtless hoping thus to swing the balance of power in her favour. Venutius waited his moment, and in A.D. 69–70 came the opportunity. The Roman world was torn with civil war, the British legions divided in loyalty, the governor unable to command them, action beyond the frontier apparently out of the question. Once more external help was forthcoming and Venutius invaded the Brigantian kingdom, where revolt was rife. Cartimandua was reduced to extremities and this time only rescued with difficulty by Roman auxiliaries. The legions did not move and the kingdom fell to Venutius.

This triumph of the anti-Roman party converted the Brigantes from a friendly buffer-state into a hostile tribe. Experience had in fact shown that Roman support could not guarantee to a client-ruler undisturbed possession. Accordingly, Vespasian's first act in Britain was to appoint a new governor, Petilius Cerealis, whose earlier legionary command had been at Lincoln, in direct contact with the disaffected area. The intention was thus clear for all to see, and Cerealis lost no time in translating it into action. The line of approach to Brigantian territory is fixed by the natural land-bridge of the Lincolnshire and Yorkshire Wolds. The Yorkshire end of the line lay through the territory of the Parisi, which embraced the East Riding. Archaeology shows that ever since the Claudian conquest this tribal area had been receptive of

Roman goods, while the later history of the tribe under
Roman rule demonstrates that their political development was more primitive than that of many British communities. In their position, wedged between the Roman
frontier and the Brigantian client-state, their choice of
adherence to Rome can never have been in doubt, and
they now, as probably before, opened the gate to Brigantia for Roman armies. Cerealis can be traced, first at
Brough, on the north bank of the Humber, later the
modest tribal capital; then at Malton, a second important
Parisian centre, from which the Vale of York can be
reached; finally, at York, where a convenient moraine
provides an easy crossing of the wide and marshy valley
and whence there is a water-way to the sea. At York was
now stationed the Ninth Legion, so that a link with the
western legions was possible; for the Twentieth, then
commanded by Agricola and probably replacing the
Fourteenth at Wroxeter, had its part to play in the conquest, now singly and now in unison. The Brigantes were
evidently assailed upon both flanks and Cerealis could
claim to have absorbed a large part of their territory by
direct conquest or by surrender. How far his forward
campaigning extended is not clear, but along one principal line of penetration it may be possible to trace his
steps. The modern main road from the Vale of York to
Carlisle follows in most places the line of its Roman pre-
decessor, which branches from the Roman north road
from Chester to Carlisle and which cannot be much later
than Agricola. Earlier still – for one of them is obliterated
by the York–Carlisle road – come three marching-camps,
big enough to hold a legion and some cavalry and of an
individual yet similar design quite different from those
associated with Agricola's troops. It is not unreasonable
to assign these three works, which cover the route from

Stainmore to Carlisle, to the army of Cerealis and in particular the Ninth Legion. Driving thus for the Solway and perhaps beyond it, Cerealis was using an age-old line of cultural and economic penetration which had been the principal channel of Brigantian expansion. The amount of early pottery at Carlisle has been thought to suggest that the grip on the Eden crossing was already more than temporary, as if an advanced post here ensured the fulfilment of terms of peace. The depth of the drive was no doubt conditioned by the existence of those external anti-Roman allies upon whom Venutius had been able to call with such effect a year or two before.

A pause could now be made in the north until the conquest of Wales was completed, a task which fell to the next governor, Iulius Frontinus. History has not preserved the earlier details of this senator's career, so that it cannot be specifically shown that previous service in Britain had given him earlier knowledge of the theatre of war. But the operations manifestly went with a swing, amid conditions much less favourable to their execution. The Silures beyond the Severn, secure in the shelter of the Forest of Dean and the foothills of the Black Mountains, had retaliated vigorously after the defeat of Caratacus in A.D. 51–2, and were thereafter contained rather than controlled. The refusal of the Second Legion to move to the aid of Paulinus in A.D. 61 must be connected with unwillingness to invite a Silurian stab in the back. Experience had in short shown that frontal penetration was on this frontier impracticable. Profiting by the example of Paulinus, Frontinus decided to use sea force and to occupy the rich and fertile sea-plain of Glamorgan. Once a foothold was here obtained the immediate result was the conquest of South Wales. Forts at the river mouths ensured command of the littoral, and the river valleys could be used to penetrate and outflank the Black Mountains and to force open the gateway to Brycheiniog by way of the upper Wye and the Usk. The importance of the Usk valley as an arterial route was emphasized by founding at Caerleon (Isca Silurum) a fortress for the Second Legion, which for long remained the seat of the south-western command. Beyond the land of the Silures the area of Caermarthenshire and Pembrokeshire belonged to the Demetae, whose territory was apparently less deeply penetrated by the strategic road-system, as if these people, probably hostile to the Silures, had welcomed rather than opposed the Romans. It cannot then have been difficult to absorb Mid-Wales between the Usk and Severn valleys, for much of the area is too wild for habitation. But north of the Severn the great wall of the Berwyns and the inner massif of Snowdonia screened and sheltered a second anti-Roman tribe, the Ordovices; and, while pushing garrisons hard against their boundaries, there Frontinus was compelled to stop. The strategical position in North Wales was not quite so easy to handle. An effective control could be operated only from a point which looked north-eastwards towards the Brigantes as well as westwards towards North Wales. This point was Chester, where it is now known that a legionary fortress was in process of erection towards the end of Frontinus' command, and that its use as a base for the conquest and organization of North Wales belongs to his successor, Iulius Agricola.

The occupation of Chester by legionaries had, however, been preceded by earlier military use of the site, which may well go back to the time of Suetonius Paulinus: for the conquest of the Flintshire Deceangli cannot be later than about this time, since their mines were producing ingots of lead in A.D. 74, by when the work of pacification and organization must be regarded as completed. As commander of the Twentieth Legion under the governor Cerealis, Agricola must already have known this region well and it is his previous knowledge of the area which explains why, on his arrival as governor, rather late in the summer of A.D. 78, he was ready to open a campaign against the Ordovices at once. Their offence was grave: they had almost annihilated a cavalry regiment stationed on their borders; and the punishment was swift and grim. Without hesitation Agricola marched a mixed punitive force up into their territory – one thinks of the major line of penetration through Cerrig-y-drudion and Bettws-y-coed – wiped out almost the whole tribe and seized Anglesey. After this it only remained to grip North Wales by forts at the river mouths and by an inner line of penetration based upon the upper Dee valley and the work of conquest was done. It was the first time in Britain that a large mountainous region had been wholly conquered and organized under military control. The arrangement provided the model for the treatment of the Brigantes and other northern tribes.

There is no doubt that it was Agricola who rounded off the consolidation of northern Britain, and that much of his work took place upon the west coast, though his hand is also traceable in County Durham and between Tyne and Solway. The next two years saw campaigns carried to the Tay and consolidation reaching the Forth–Clyde isthmus, where a temporary line of forts and fortlets barred out any counter-move. The main task had been the envelopment and penetration of the territory of the Selgovae, who occupied the entire basin of the middle and upper Tweed. The coastal tribe of the Votadini, stretching from Northumberland to the Forth, also came into the net, though without so strong a garrison and therefore

Figure 2

perhaps with more goodwill. Only when these areas were settled could Agricola turn his attention westwards and consider the problem of Galloway and its relation to Ireland. Until air-photography and excavation recently showed otherwise, it was thought that the Roman attitude towards Galloway was to shun it. Now it is evident that not only Galloway but Ayrshire was penetrated by Roman forces and dominated by permanent forts. This explains why Agricola should have considered with such vivid longing the conquest of Ireland and, conversely,

why an Irish chieftain should have pinned his hopes upon
Roman backing. Only those who have viewed the opposite coasts from either Larne or Portpatrick can realize
how imminent the threat of conquest or how bright the
opportunity must have seemed. On balance, however,
the negative decision then taken was wise, when related
to Roman resources in manpower, and none of the considerations arising on the spot outweighs that factor.

The year spent in consolidation behind the temporary frontier on the Forth–Clyde Isthmus was also used
in giving consideration to the prospects beyond it. It was
doubtless at this time that Agricola explored the west
coast and its islands with the fleet, seconding the school-
master Demetrius of Tarsus to the party of exploration.
Geographical inquiry was the prime purpose of the
expedition, but its strategical aim must have been more
special, namely to determine whether there was any way
of circumventing or outflanking the Highland plateau.
Previous reconnaissance, before the temporary line of the
Forth–Clyde Isthmus was chosen, must have revealed
that this was the cardinal problem which remained, and
the action now taken by Agricola shows that he judged
an outflanking move to be impossible. No such action as
had taken place in South Wales was going to prove
feasible in Scotland. The strategy now planned and skilfully applied during the next two years was to gain firm
possession of Strathmore, the gateway to the north, to
deny to northern attackers the use of it as a springboard,
and then to provoke the northern tribes to a pitched
battle of such a scale that defeat would cripple them for
at least a generation or longer. That is the meaning of the
final operations of Agricola and their culmination in the
great battle of Mons Graupius, which was a victory comparable with the later Culloden. The result was to leave

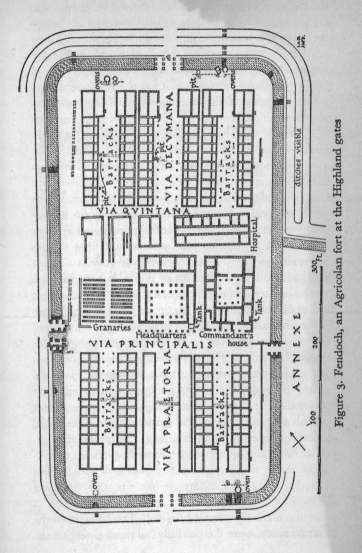

Figure 3. Fendoch, an Agricolan fort at the Highland gates

the Romans in possession of all lowland Scotland, with Highland resistance broken. On the strength of this notable achievement Agricola was recalled in A.D. 84, after a longer governorship than the normal, and the Flavian forward movement was at an end.

If archaeology provided, as it has not yet done, a basis for an estimate of the number of auxiliary regiments employed in garrisoning the Claudio-Neronian frontiers in Britain, it would be possible to assess the extra strain placed upon the British garrison as the result of the Flavian forward movement. But if area counts for anything, the increase in territory policed by military troops as a result of the Flavian conquests was very great. The previous frontier, comprising the Fosse Way, its hinterland, and its fringe, even if that fringe extended up to or beyond the Severn, hardly covers more than Wales demanded, while the northern frontier covered about two and a half times the area of Wales. But the increase was no isolated phenomenon: and the forward movement had gone ahead elsewhere on the frontiers of the Empire in response to similar needs of straightening out awkward salients and re-entrants or eliminating unreliable buffer States. The reverse side of the picture was the contribution in manpower which the newly-annexed areas could make, the quota of one area going to form the garrison of another. In this respect Britain had an important contribution to make to the grand scheme of Imperial defence, a living tribute which might be judged to make worth while the counter-expenditure in garrisons.

But while thus lavish in its increase of the Roman auxiliary army the Flavian age made no corresponding increase in the legions. These formidable shock troops, at once the crack fighters and the skilled technicians of the Roman army, were the carefully balanced pieces on the chess-board of Empire and their number was not even slightly increased without the weightiest reasons. The very conception of a balance of power between the different regions of the Empire dictated, too, that there should be no mobile reserve of legions to disturb it. Consequently, when pressure fell heavily upon a given frontier, the sole means of substantial reinforcement was the stripping of others. When, therefore, pressure began to bear heavily upon the Danube frontier in the later eighties, it was felt politic to deprive Britain of a legion for service in Pannonia. The fact that this legion, on duty in the far north, was vital to the Agricolan scheme of British defences could be of no weight against danger on the frontier nearest to the heart of the Empire.

The legion chosen for Central Europe was II Adiutrix, largely raised in Pannonia, which had come to Britain in A.D. 71 and had been stationed first at Lincoln and then at Chester. The Chester position, however, had to be filled whatever happened further north. Until now the northern permanent defences had consisted of the Inchtuthil fortress and a line of forts blocking the Highland passes from Bochastle, near Callander, to Stracathro, near Edzell. The fortress and at least one fort, at Fendoch in Glenalmond, were now abandoned and this carries with it all positions north of the Earn. But the grip upon Strathearn held firm and the organization of defence in the Lowlands was now pivoted upon Newstead, where a great and massive reconstruction of the fort took place and legionaries and auxiliaries were brigaded together. There is no sign of the slackening of this grip until about A.D. 100, when all the forts north of the Cheviot and perhaps north of the Tyne–Solway gap were evacuated. But whether this contraction of commitments was due to increasing enemy pressure or to a deliberate attempt to reduce the British

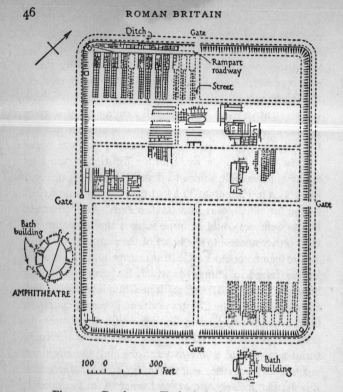

Figure 4. Caerleon, a Trajanic legionary fortress

garrison still further is not apparent. All that can be said is that it coincided with a firm consolidation of legionary fortresses and forts further south. The process seems to have begun at Caerleon in A.D. 99 and to have spread thence to auxiliary forts throughout Wales. It is discernible at Chester after A.D. 102 and at York in A.D. 107–8: but it is not so certain how far it extended to the forts of the north, for many reconstructions in stone which were once thought to fit the consolidation of Trajan now prove to be linked with activity at the end of the reign of Antoninus Pius. At Corbridge, for example, one of the biggest and most important forts in the north, there is no pre-Antonine reconstruction of the site in stone.

The consolidation of the military area in Britain under Trajan is a corollary of his intense contemporary activity in Dacia, where British auxiliary regiments played a gallant part, and of his later campaigns in the Orient. But the silence which ensued is due to lack of sources and not to proved tranquillity. Certain it is that very soon after Trajan's death in A.D. 117 trouble came which involved heavy legionary casualties and which Fronto, two generations later, remembered as especially severe. This is to be connected with the issue of victory coins in A.D. 119 and the fact that by A.D. 122 the Ninth Legion was replaced at York by the Sixth and disappeared from the army lists thereafter. That the Legion was cashiered, there is no doubt, and it seems evident that this fate, at the hands of the disciplinarian Hadrian, followed an ignominious defeat. But the unit was not annihilated. Some of its officers at least survived and nothing whatever is reported of the circumstances or place of the trouble. The steps which Hadrian took to repair the damage suggest, however, that the seat of disturbance lay in south-western Scotland.

This great consolidator of the Empire took in Britain, as elsewhere, an engineer's view of the problem. The work of Augustus, who chose natural barriers for the Imperial frontiers, was to be supplemented by artificial barriers where required, and of these Hadrian's Wall in Britain, between Tyne and Solway, was at once the shortest and the most impressive in scale and in siting. Beginning, as first planned, at Pons Aelius (Newcastle upon Tyne) and choosing the shortest route from sea to sea south of the Cheviot, it grips the northern rim of the Tyne and Irthing valleys and terminates on the southern shore of the Solway beyond its lowest ford. The whole barrier was at first seventy-six Roman miles long. The eastern forty-five miles were closed by a wall of stone, designed ten Roman feet wide and fifteen high to parapet walk, the western thirty-one by a rampart of turf, twenty Roman feet wide at the base and some twelve feet high. The barriers were fronted, wherever needed, by a great ditch and were patrolled from attached fortlets, or mile-castles, placed at every Roman mile, with two turrets between them. These parts of the defences were designed to prevent infiltration. The second problem was the defence against attacks. For this purpose each milecastle was provided with a wide sally-port, through any of which the fighting garrisons stationed behind the Wall might issue to encircle attackers and drive them against the barrier, like hunters using a corral. Thus employed, Roman disciplined tactics and superior equipment could be made to tell. But such a tactical disposition could be put into action much better if the fighting garrison was placed upon the Wall itself and this was the sense of an important change of plan, carried out while the work was still under construction. The Wall was supplied in stages with its sixteen well-known forts, covering all main lines of approach, and was itself extended eastwards from Newcastle to Wallsend, increasing its length to eighty Roman miles. Once this change took place the entire work could be marked off from its wild hinterland by a continuous cleared strip or *limes*, known as the Vallum, bordered by mounds and made into a formidable obstacle by a deep flat-bottomed ditch running along its axis. All that then remained was to replace the turf rampart by a rampart of stone. This substitution had already begun during the fort-building, when the stone wall from North Tyne to a point five miles west of the Irthing had been erected at a thickness reduced to eight Roman feet, and the vast building programme ended in a final extension of the work in stone throughout Cumberland. Two subsidiary provisions remain to be mentioned. The west flank of the system was protected for over thirty miles by equipping the Cumberland shore with milefortlets and towers, organized like the milecastles and turrets of the Wall but unconnected by a barrier. Secondly, the Cumbrian approaches, including the Solway fords, were screened by outpost-forts at Bewcastle, Netherby, and Birrens. These provisions appear to belong to the original scheme.

The great work was thus at length finished. Construction began in A.D. 122 or 123: the work on the forts was completed not very long after A.D. 128. It seems certain that the first designers did not intend the task to have taken so long: certain also that the additions to the scheme imply a mounting intensity of attack upon the barrier and a need to keep unwanted folk on the south away from the military zone. But the changes can also be viewed as an adaptation of what was already there to local circumstances which the original designers had not appreciated accurately.

The unforeseen degree of pressure which the Wall had to withstand attests the irritation which this application of the new type of closed frontier caused among the excluded tribesmen. On the Roman side the scheme undoubtedly resulted in some economy of manpower. Wales seems to have contributed its quota of troops to supply the Wall-garrison, and in the hinterland of the Wall there was some reorganization of garrisons. But the external pressure and internal economy were soon considered together

in another fashion. Pressure could be reduced if Lowland
Scotland were reoccupied: manpower expenditure would
not be increased if the Pennines and Wales could be further
denuded of troops. Again, the reservoir of fighting Britons
now potentially, and perhaps actually, so vexatious to
defenders of the Wall could be drained away and drafted
for service in another province with great advantage to
the Imperial budget of manpower.

Some such thoughts as these seem to have influenced
the next phase of Imperial policy in Britain, which was
a swing from the Hadrianic recession to a forward
movement. The new advance put into practice few
novel conceptions. Agricola's line from Forth to Clyde
was reoccupied, and was stiffened by a new frontier
in the Hadrianic manner, with modifications of some
interest due to experience. There was no rearward
Vallum; a larger ditch was dug in front of the Wall,
which is turf-built but equally steep and hard to scale at
back and front. The forts are smaller and more closely
spaced, so that smaller garrisons might more quickly and
in closer concert round up the enemy against the barrier
and its great ditch. Turrets are unknown, but more than
one structure like a milecastle has been found between
forts. Tactically considered, the Antonine Wall was in fact
less an imitation of the great work which it superseded than
a skilfully devised improvement upon it. Strategically it
is more open to criticism. Its flanks are weak, and the
weakness is emphasized by the precautions taken to avoid
it. All Fife had to be encircled in order to prevent its use
as a spring-board for an attack on the east. The western
precautions are less certain, but they include arrangements for patrolling the south bank of the Clyde estuary,
where this flank is weakest; and a fortified approach-road
through the pass of Darvel implies an occupation of the

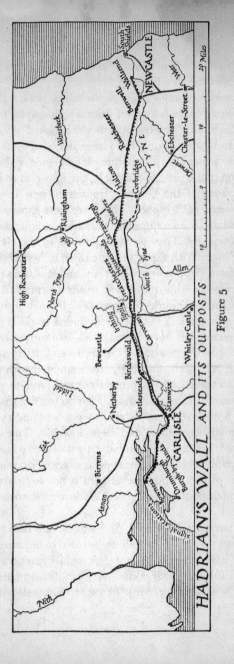

HADRIAN'S WALL AND ITS OUTPOSTS

Figure 5

Ayrshire coast, whence the distance to free Kintyre seems
a stone's throw on a fine day.

The conscious imitation of Agricola's tactics is reflected
in a telling phrase borrowed from his biography to describe the work. 'The barbarians were moved up', as it
were into another island. The phrase has been connected,
probably wrongly, with another consequence of the new
extension of the province, namely, the appearance in the
Neckar zone of the German frontier of new irregular
detachments of Brittones. These are best explained as
levies exacted from conquered tribes who had surrendered
unconditionally. They were established in the German
frontier area. With them, to settle them in, went officials
drawn from the provincial garrison and it was no doubt
such overseers who introduced to the German frontier
fashions in stonework recognizably derived from the
British command. A hint of the denuded land, its populace depleted but not exterminated, is afforded by the
disposition of the garrison of the hinterland. It lay now in
widely spaced forts, linked by roads studded with small
posts, intended both to protect convoys and to check
unauthorized movement. And it is noteworthy that the
system is most evident in south-west Scotland, where
anti-Roman aggression had been heaviest. The wide-
spacing of the main garrison indicates a depleted and dis-
armed populace: the frequent posts denote rigorous and
watchful control. The arrangement is not so unlike the
Highland dispositions of General Wade after the conquest
of 1745.

The barrier of Hadrian's Wall was for the time being
thrown open freely. The Wall itself ceased to be patrolled;
only its forts were held, often by less mobile garrisons; the
doors of the milecastle gateways were dismantled; the
Vallum was furnished with frequent unimpeded cross-

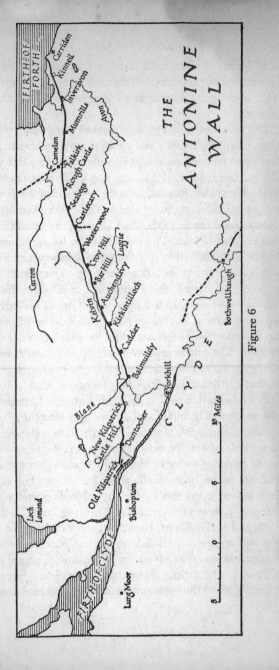

THE ANTONINE WALL

FIRTH OF FORTH

Carriden
Kinneil
Inveravon
Mumrills
Avon
Camelon
Falkirk
Rough Castle
Seabegs
Castlecary
Westerwood
Croy Hill
Bar Hill
Auchendavy
Lurggie
Kirkintilloch
Cadder
Balmuildy
Yorkhill

Carron
Kelvin

Blane
New Kilpatrick
Castle Hill
Duntocher
Old Kilpatrick
Bishopton

Loch Lomond

FIRTH OF CLYDE

Lurg Moor

CLYDE

Bothwellhaugh

Figure 6

5   0   5   10 Miles

ings. Among the Brigantes forts were freely scrapped, as
if with the advancement of the frontier a new age of
peace had begun. But it was not long before the situation
changed.

The revolt of A.D. 155–8 is marked partly by reconstructions and partly by records of troop movements. An
important fort was rebuilt at Birrens and a new fort was
planted on a deserted Flavian site at Brough (Derbyshire). Birrens lies forward from the west end of the Tyne–
Solway gap; Brough, succeeded by the modern Castleton,
is the natural centre of the Peak District, exploited for its
rich supplies of lead. The two places lie too far apart to
assume without further proof that the land between them
was aflame with revolt. But the troop movements help
to fill in the picture; reinforcements for all three British
legions were landed in the Tyne, direct from the German
provinces, and at Corbridge a dedication by an officer of
the Sixth Legion attests casualties for which revenge was
exacted. The concentration of activity on the Tyne is
surely significant of a determination to hold firmly the
southern isthmus as a base for operations further north
and of a hesitation to operate freely until reinforcements
had arrived. A Roman would have said that they 'held
a wolf by the ears', a stalemate only to be relieved by
help from outside. What seems certain is the temporary
loss of territory north of Hadrian's Wall. What is more
doubtful is the state of affairs further south: but some
light is shed upon this by further rebuilding under the
governor Calpurnius Agricola at Corbridge and Chesterholm, and at Hardknott, Lancaster, and Ribchester in the
west and at Ilkley and Bainbridge in the Pennines, with a
re-occupation also at Melandra near Glossop, neighbour
to Brough. This clearly shows that in the upland parts of
Brigantia, amid the forests and fells of Cumberland, north

Lancashire, and the Pennines, there had been sufficient unrest to call for re-occupation.

The consequence of this situation was a temporary evacuation of the Scottish Wall and the Lowland forts, and, when re-occupation came, a simultaneous holding of Hadrian's Wall as well. Much shuffling of garrisons was needed to effect this, and in the zone beyond the Forth–Clyde isthmus forts were reduced in size, while traces of similar measures to save manpower are discernible in lesser degree in the land behind it. These measures too are almost certainly to be ascribed to Calpurnius Agricola, but the direct proof afforded by inscriptions is lacking. But at all excavated sites north of Hadrian's Wall evidence for a reconstruction of about this time has been found: and it is reasonable to link it with the better-documented series of reconstructions, which cannot in any case have been isolated. One of the new measures deserves special note. Newstead, the great fort which was the pivot of activity in the Lowlands, received a larger cavalry garrison than ever before, an *ala* one thousand strong. These costly and valuable regiments, almost rarer than the legions, were habitually placed upon frontiers where attacks in force, which called for a rapid and decisive repulse, might be made on a fairly wide front. The change suggests, firstly, that the northern territory was yielding enough to make its retention desirable and, secondly, that thrusts of some strength had been probing for weak spots in its defences.

The next record of disturbance in the north, in the opening years of the Emperor Commodus, mentions just such a thrust and its authors, the barbarians beyond the Wall. They broke through and did serious damage, killing a legate and his men. There is no disturbance of the period on Hadrian's Wall and the Antonine Wall must

be meant. The disaster was also followed by a sharp punitive campaign under Ulpius Marcellus. Whether the
damage extended to the whole Scottish Wall is uncertain,
but the third period of occupation detected in many of
its forts is best explicable as of this time.

Whatever actually happened, an event occurred at the
close of the century which must unquestionably coincide
with a break in the occupation of the northern frontier.
In A.D. 193, when Commodus had been assassinated and
the line of Imperial succession was broken, Septimius
Severus, governor of Moesia, used his army to make himself Emperor. Others were ready to do the same. Pescen-
nius Niger, governor of Syria, and Clodius Albinus,
governor of Britain, were both rival claimants, and
Severus, playing one off against the other, recognized
Albinus as Caesar, or heir-apparent, in order to gain
time. But Albinus was in fact preparing for a civil war
with the support of the army of Britain, and when Severus
broke off relations in A.D. 196 Albinus was ready to trans-
fer much of his army to the Continent, leaving the northern defences empty or weakened to breaking point behind
him. There was no turning back and the army felt it; in
two battles, the second decisive, the army of Britain,
using with deadly effect its leaden missiles, almost won
the day. When it was beaten, the province went to the
victor.

It was a wasted military heritage into which Severus
entered. On the news of the defeat of Albinus, the northern tribes had broken in, plundering and burning.
Almost every excavated fort between York and the north
shows traces of destruction at this time, and the walls of
York had to be rebuilt from their foundations, though
the fortress at Chester stood unscathed. Strong military
action at once was out of the question. The raiders were

bought off and time was thus gained for the reconstruction of the base of York and of the wasted forts, hardly less than thirty in number from Hadrian's Wall southwards. As a whole the work took time. The forts of Yorkshire and Stainmore were put in hand within a year: but work was still in progress in the rest of the area, and in Yorkshire too, almost a decade later, under the governors of A.D. 205–8. By that date, however, Hadrian's Wall was rebuilt, together with the outpost forts beyond it, now extended to cover Northumberland as well as the western approaches to the Wall. Further, the governor Alfenus Senecio was operating beyond and winning victories in A.D. 206. However, his report summing up the situation at this time was realistic enough. 'The need was either more troops to reinforce the frontier area, or an Imperial expedition.'

In terms of earlier events and previous treatment of the problem the meaning of this report is unmistakable. The aggressors were the Maeatae of Strathmore and Strathearn, who later became the southern part of the Pictish nation. In the past they had been held in check by Roman occupation of at least the southern portion of their territory, and the need to control them or their movements had brought the Romans into the lower Tay basin. If that were done again, and if a great expedition could also be mounted against the northern tribes, the settled conditions so seriously disrupted in A.D. 197 might return. Severus chose this Agricolan policy, partly to get his two sons away from the capital, much more to give them the experience in organization that they required and to prepare them for joint rule in due course. Thus, on the coins of Caracalla, who had been joint Augustus since the defeat of Albinus, preparations for the British expedition are so prominently heralded as to raise the question whether

Caracalla was not already in the province by A.D. 207. It was, however, in A.D. 208 that Severus, his Empress, and Geta arrived in Britain, and Severus began with Caracalla the year of preparation for a northern campaign which at once induced the tribes concerned to beg, in vain, for peace. When the year was over the attack was delivered not against the Maeatae but against the Caledonians. The measures taken were remarkable. Not only was Cramond on the Firth of Forth reoccupied, but a new legionary fortress, holding some six cohorts of the Sixth Legion, honoured with the title *Britannica*, was erected at Carpow on the Tay above Abernethy. A return was thus made to the Agricolan principle of covering Strathmore with a large force. The choice of Carpow explains why much preparation of roads was undertaken in marshy country, a description suitable to Fife or the lower Earn valley but hardly to the long-established land-route between Forth and Tay, which would require no more than refurbishing. The rare *Traiectus* coin of Caracalla, commemorating the crossing of Forth or Tay on a bridge of boats, marks the opening of the expedition, rapid and thorough. The Caledonians were beaten into unconditional surrender, with laying down of arms and contribution of levies. It is worth while to emphasize that the ceremony of surrender took place in Caledonia and that this was more than any other Roman conqueror ever achieved. The next winter, however, the Maeatae flared into revolt, and had themselves to be punished by a further campaign, while a winter later both groups broke into revolt again, and were only saved from a war of extermination by the death of Severus in February, A.D. 211. One further campaign followed, suppressed by historians hostile to Caracalla but attested by the coins, and peace-terms were then laid down, while Caracalla

withdrew all Roman garrisons to the line of Hadrian's
Wall and its forward zone. The undertaking which the
Maeatae and Caledonians had broken was not to unite
in common action. This at least must have been insisted
upon; while, if the campaign was originally undertaken
to protect the lands north of Hadrian's Wall, a coherent
picture of the new arrangement begins to emerge. The
northern tribes, soon to be known as Picts but at this time
divided into two groups, were to abstain from raiding their
Brythonic neighbours south of the Forth. The Brythonic
tribes, until recently enveloped within the Empire, were
still to be protected but left without garrisons, much
as the Frisii or the Hermunduri were treated on the
Rhine or Danube. For the better control of their territory, the new outpost-forts of Hadrian's Wall were
equipped with large and semi-mobile garrisons, and
became also the headquarters for irregular units of
exploratores or frontier patrol-men. The occupied zone
of the new model frontier thus extended not merely to
the Cheviot, but its patrols ranged still further afield, to
Lothian, Upper Clydesdale, or Galloway. This implies a
measure of regulated control of the Lowland tribes which
is echoed in the list of their authorized meeting-places
or *loca*, recently recognized to exist in the geographical
document known as the Ravenna Cosmography. It is
indicated also in the character of the new native settlements, devoid of formidable defences and frequently lacking any defence at all. Here may be recognized the con-
trolling hand of Rome, which guaranteed peace and
allowed barriers only against wild beasts and chance
marauders. Very similar arrangements are discernible in
Wales, where the native fortifications of the period are of
the same type, civil defences rather than military works.

The dispositions of Caracalla thus deserve more credit

than they have often received. They guaranteed peace in northern Britain for longer than the action of any other Roman general ever enforced it; and they seem to have achieved this despite the serious worsening of political and economic conditions that afflicted the Empire during the frequent collapses of central authority in the middle and later years of the third century A.D. It would seem that it was Caracalla also who built the first coastal fort, at Reculver, against Pictish and Saxon sea-raids.

The growing danger from Saxon pirates has left its traces at Richborough, where, in the last quarter of the third century A.D., the lofty triumphal monument commemorating the conquest of the island was girt by ditches and converted into a look-out post. The system seems to have been related to warning the fleet of approaching hostile craft, with a view to their interception. Interception was certainly the basic tactical idea, whether the pirates were caught on the way in or the way out, for these are the operations described in the career of Carausius, the admiral of the *classis Britannica*. It was an accusation that he waited too often for the return journey of the pirates, and shared their booty with them, that led to his act of usurpation. Rather than face a trial, Carausius seized Britain and the Low Countries and had himself proclaimed Augustus. His island Empire, recognized for a while by central authority, lasted for six years, when he was assassinated by his chief finance officer, Allectus, who was not overcome for another three. During these nine years (A.D. 287–96) Carausius and Allectus began the series of coastal defences known as the Saxon Shore. These works, partly embodying old-style forts, such as Reculver and Brancaster, and partly built to the new pattern, based upon elaborate town defences, ran from Norfolk to the Isle of Wight. They held mixed garrisons

of soldiers and sailors, for intercepting raiders both by
land and sea, and they could be used in combination
as bases for sea-patrols. Nor were such foundations
confined to the south-east coast of the island. On the
west coast they are, indeed, much less well known: but
examples occur at Cardiff and at Lancaster and these
cannot have stood alone. It is probable, however, that
the western examples, and some of the Saxon Shore forts
too, belong to the restoration of Constantius I, who re-
united the island to the Empire in A.D. 296. His victory,
like that of Severus, cost him the northern frontier, which
had been stripped of troops and which was invaded and
wasted when Allectus was defeated. This time the damage
was worse, for it included Chester as well as York, as if
the Scotti of Northern Ireland were now among the sea-
raiders by whom the island was threatened. But with
Roman constancy and pertinacity the damage was
repaired and in good fashion. York, indeed, rose statelier
than ever before, with a fortress whose river-front was a
grandiose version of the newest style in military architecture: while the land approaches to the Vale of York were
dominated by new forts of great size holding mounted
garrisons big enough to hunt down and overwhelm even
the largest raiding bands. The new prosperity of the area,
of which more will be said in a later chapter (p. 119), is
an indication of the success of these vigorous measures.

The sea-patrols of the period deserve special mention,
since they gained a place in classical literature. Vegetius,
who dedicated his work to Valentinian I (A.D. 364–75),
describes the contemporary scout-ships. They were fast,
light craft, their hulls and rigging painted sea-green and
their crew of twenty rowers clad in sea-green clothing.
They were named *pictae*, presumably because they resembled Pictish curraghs (*curucae*), and their task was not

to engage enemy ships but to report their movements to the Roman fleet.

The most eloquent testimony to the general success of these measures was the reaction which in due time they prompted. After some sixty years of frustration the barbarians, among whom concerted action was so rare as to lie outside Roman reckoning, resorted to a great joint attack. In A.D. 367 the Saxons, Picts, and Scots made a synchronized assault upon the province, killing the Count of the Saxon Shore, who was head of coastal defence, and immobilizing the Duke of the Britains, who was commander-in-chief of inland forces. The Wall and the forts of the north again fell, and it is recorded that the cause of this item in the chapter of disaster was the treachery of the frontier scouts, who were bought over by promises of a share in the loot. There were also many cases of desertion.

When the storm was over and Count Theodosius, bringing numerous new troops with him, had restored order, it was a different frontier world that arose in the north. Until now the Wall had been garrisoned by troops organized in regular regiments, however territorialized such units may have become through local recruiting or through hereditary obligations to army service. The Wall forts had attracted substantial extramural civil settlements, especially where, as at Housesteads (Borcovicium), there was an established market for trade beyond the frontier. Now that those settlements had perished amid fire and slaughter they were not renewed. The new garrisons, with their women and children, lived exclusively within the forts, crudely reconstructed by provincial labour. The forts thus became little fortified townships, more like a medieval Conway, Beaumaris, or Flint than a Roman *castellum*, and in medieval fashion the garrisons received the surrounding land to cultivate in return for their services. How such organization, or lack of it, played havoc with the internal disposition of buildings still arranged on traditional lines is revealed at not a few forts, where granaries became dwellings and headquarters buildings became half store-houses and half living-quarters. A centurion of the old order would have blenched at the sight.

Such garrisons as these, farmer-soldiers no longer at the old pitch of readiness, could not be given the task of patrolling the outlands, where the old patrol-system had in any case broken down. To meet the new situation, the tribes of the outlands, who had grown in political experience under Roman tutelage, were given increased independence, and converted from protectorates into *foederati* or treaty states. The two groups were the Damnonii of Strathclyde and the Votadini of Lothian and Northumberland, the later Bernicia, whose native dynasties have authentic pedigrees going back to this period and also names and titles which suggest Roman influence and Roman suzerainty. This may be regarded as the good fruit yielded by the policy of Caracalla, which first converted the south of Scotland into protectorates that were in reality buffer states.

Elsewhere than in the furthest north new measures continued to be taken. The best known example is on the Yorkshire coast, which was equipped with up-to-date fortlets containing great towers to espy and to signal the approach of sea-raiders and so to set naval operations in train for their interception. Some forts, again, were re-occupied, as, for example, Caernarvon in North Wales, adjacent to copper deposits of considerable value. At Caer Gybi, Holyhead, a fortified beaching-point was built for warships, matching those used for contemporary

Rhine and Danube flotillas. There is every indication
that a firm hold was kept upon the nerve-centre of the
north at York and upon the large inland forts connected
therewith, such as Malton and Piercebridge. These and
the naval ports were the bases from which the long arm
of Rome could still strike. After A.D. 367 a naval repair-
depot was still operating in the Bristol Channel; and it
must be significant that the very last offensive measures
in Britain, ascribed by a Roman writer to Stilicho, were
naval raids following the usurpation of Magnus Maximus
of A.D. 383–8. Whether these actually took place or not,
the fruits of comparable action on the part of the Roman
government may be clearly recognized in the regiments
of Scotti and Atecotti forming part of the Continental
army of the Emperor Honorius. These represent levies
from overseas outside the British province, either exacted
after offensive action or bought by Roman gold, but in
any case relieving pressure upon the coasts of Britain. The
Scotti came from Northern Ireland and the Atecotti
probably from the western littoral of Scotland.

If the final stages of defence and the new devolution of
responsibility for it in the north can thus be traced with
some approach to the truth, the position in other parts of
the island is less sure. But it is important for an understanding of the latest phase of Romano-British military
activity on the East Coast that East Anglia and the East
Riding adjacent to York are filled now with late-Roman
pottery in Saxon taste and now with some of the earliest
Saxon cemeteries in Britain, comparable with those of
the late fourth and early fifth century A.D. on the Continent. It suggests very strongly that Honorius, if not his
predecessors, had adopted for Britain the policy of settling
folk of the outlands, in this case Saxons, in the border
territories of the Empire which they had once come to

rob, giving them lands in exchange for military service. The precise bearing of this upon Saxon settlement in Britain cannot as yet be documented or traced. But it at least places the tradition of Hengist and Horsa in a continuity, making the event less isolated and more comprehensible. Vortigern's action can be seen as forming part of the pattern of devolution rather than as a new remedy by a desperate and inexperienced native prince.

CHAPTER TWO

TOWNS AND URBAN CENTRES

THE military history of Roman Britain derives not a little of its interest from the variety and ingenuity of its pattern, which stamps it as a lively and vigorous reaction to Imperial problems, now external and now internal. But the basic assumption behind all such action is that there was a province worth protection, a land which paid dividends in either taxation, or troops, or raw materials; these yields were sufficient, singly or in combination, to justify an occupation on grounds of expense, quite apart from the over-riding strategical considerations which originally and continually made the occupation desirable. An occupation, furthermore, in conferring peace and order, brought about the conditions in which population and productivity might be substantially increased. The tribute yield of the Three Gauls was doubled in fifty years, and while the expansion cannot have continued at so prodigious a rate, it remains a valuable indication of what might happen in the first tide of peace and prosperity among people who did not welcome the new order with unanimity.

The instrument of civilization used by Rome in achieving such results was the town and the many-sided attainments of amenity and social grace which successful civic organization involves. No false modesty or feeling for others inhibited the Roman belief in their own hybrid civilization, though they enjoyed analysing its shams and pretences with the scorn of a quick-witted and confident race. The normal method of introducing the instrument in Celtic lands, where the most important political unit was the council of jealous tribal notables, was through the aristocratic families. These were encouraged to adopt Roman ways and to give their sons a Roman education, absorbing these things as the inward stamp of a new civilization whose outward habits and equipment possessed the magnetism of novelty and the prestige of success. Once this movement got under way the rest would follow. Tribal revenues, private generosity, and family pride or emulation could be devoted to creating an urban centre for tribal government, tribal festivals, and tribal markets, which had meanwhile been left undisturbed by the Roman provincial administration as far as was compatible with its needs. At this stage the Roman government lent a hand. The development was not permitted until the financial soundness of the proposal had been examined and approved. Then a surveyor or architect might be lent and a new town or local government centre would begin to rise, with its lands duly apportioned and its streets laid off in Roman manner.

But to suppose that this happened in the first years of development of the province is to go too fast. The earliest phase of Romano-British tribal capitals is much more modest and begins with traders gathered at the tribal centre, in simple timber shacks and workshops. Such agglomerations have been noted under Claudius at Verulamium (St Albans), Durovernum Cantiorum (Canterbury), and Ratae Coritanorum (Leicester), the first as ribbon development along a Roman road. This is a natural growth, matched at early Gallic capitals such as Bibracte (Mont Beuvray). Meanwhile, those who might further such matters had to learn what a Roman town was like. In a new overseas province this was difficult, and it was not until seven years after the invasion that the

governor Ostorius Scapula set about founding and building such a place on the site of the capital of Cunobelinus
at Camulodunum (Colchester). The primary object of
the foundation was to provide a chartered town or *colonia*
for veteran legionaries, who would receive a house-plot
in the town and an amount of cultivable land outside it
appropriate to their rank. But in such foundations local
inhabitants might also share within defined limits, and
it is clear that the Trinovantes had a place at Camulodunum. Towns of the kind, with their sewered streets in
ordered rectangular plan, imposing public buildings,
comfortable private houses, and a good town-hall were
not erected quickly. Twenty or twenty-five years might
well elapse from start to finish, and the order of building
the several elements varied. At Camulodunum after
eleven years a senate-house, theatre, and private dwellings existed, but work on the town defences had not yet
begun. Above all, much time had been spent upon erecting the Temple of Claudius which was to be the centre of
Emperor-worship for the whole province. Roman historians remarked, looking back upon these events, how
amenities had come first: and this is comprehensible,
when the political and cultural education of the native
aristocracy was the first and fundamental condition of
civilizing the province as a whole.

How the cult of the Emperor could take its place in the
scheme needs explanation. In Rome and among Roman
citizens the world over, the living Emperor was the first
citizen, deriving his power and authority from the
Senate; only after death was an Emperor of good repute
deified. But among the lower orders of citizens, the over-
whelming power and prestige of the Emperor led to his
receiving divine honours while alive, and in higher circles
also the same reaction was frequent enough. To this view,

in more extravagant form, the eastern half of the Empire, long used to the idea of semi-divine kingship, needed no conversion. In the west, where the Emperor had sole charge of almost every province beyond the Alps, the idea was employed politically. The tribes of free Gaul had been wont to meet in a sacred annual convention to discuss common interests and to perform common rites. When Druidism was forbidden by Rome, on the ground of its abhorrent human sacrifices, the annual tribal meeting was reconstituted at the new provincial capital under the auspices of Rome and Augustus. The tribes elected from among themselves a priest and priestess to hold office for a year, maintaining the calendared ritual and presiding over the great annual festival of games and contests in literature and music. But the new proceedings were conducted in Latin, for the honour and welfare of the Roman state, and the festival thus became a focus of loyalty and Romanization. The Claudian plan was to establish a similar institution for Britain centred at Camulodunum. For several reasons the venture was not a success. It was not founded upon tradition, for the British tribes held no common meeting; it was probably too sharp a transition; it was certainly too costly a burden, because it fell too often upon too few tribes. Finally, it chose for its object of devotion not Rome and the Emperor, a conception sufficiently august to survive political mischances, but Claudius himself, whose court and administration were notorious no less for their corruption than for his failure to perceive it. This explains why, in certain quarters, the venture bred discontent and disillusionment rather than comprehension and enthusiasm. The revolt of A.D. 60, in which the new *colonia* perished in flames and its inhabitants in massacre or torture, was in part fed upon local revulsion towards a cult which had made a bad psychological start and was proving too heavy an economic burden.

British communities had thus to find their own way towards a civilization which attracted them at first by its convenience rather than by its subjective qualities. How the start was made in many has already been indicated. But there is one town which introduces another political gradation, namely, the capital of a kingdom which was left to itself as an independent unit within the province and even granted sovereignty over other tribes. This was the realm of Cogidumnus; it was known as Regnum, and its folk as the Regnenses. The territory lay in a significant position, on the left flank of the first Roman advance upon the Thames, and on the right flank of their second advance, against the Belgae of Wiltshire and the Durotriges of Dorset. Further, the study of pre-Claudian native coins in Britain seems to show clearly enough that the area was threatened by both the groups whom the Romans were attacking and that it had formerly belonged to the pro-Roman Verica. Whether Cogidumnus, its ruler under Claudius, was a descendant of Verica is quite unknown. But it is certain that he became a Roman client-king on the initial organization of the province and it may well prove that his territory was the springboard for legate Vespasian's attack upon the west, which captured the Isle of Wight and subdued two great tribes. His capital, Noviomagus (Chichester), has yielded two remarkable inscriptions, one lost, the other preserved, which illustrate the duties of a client-king. The lost piece was a dedication in honour of the Emperor Nero, dated to either A.D. 58 or 60. The text is an elaborate statement of his Imperial ancestry and expressed with punctilious accuracy the reverence which a subject king was expected to have for his lord the Emperor. The second stone, which is not dated, is a dedication of a temple to Neptune and Minerva by a guild of iron-workers on the authority of Cogidumnus, who is described as *Tiberius Claudius Cogidumnus, rex et legatus Augusti in Britannia*. This unique title implies that Cogidumnus had been endowed not only with Roman citizenship but with legatine authority within the province equivalent to that of a legionary legate, who had the insignia of a praetor, the second grade of senatorial magistrates. At the other side of the Roman world King Herod Agrippa had received comparable insignia, but not the legatine authority; and it is this conferment of Roman rank which attests in remarkable fashion the confidence felt in Cogidumnus by the Imperial Government, which had placed more than one other tribe under his rule. The rest of the inscription indicates his efforts to foster, as became a client-king, the Romanization of his realm. This is demonstrated by the dedication to Roman deities, first the god of the sea over which the Wealden iron was brought to Chichester, and then the goddess of the craft which fashioned it, by the iron-workers' guild organized in Roman style: and, above all, by the wording of the text in solemn Roman legal diction. Structural remains of the period are not yet known at this native prince's capital. But the inscriptions are for Britain a rare and valuable documentation of the activities of its principal philo-Roman prince. They indicate how much might be done upon the initiative of a single potentate.

By the last quarter of the century ambitions were growing larger and the credit for their development is given by Tacitus to Agricola, though he also knew that this intelligent governor was not in fact the first to take advantage of the current tendency. It is to this period that the street systems of Isca Dumnoniorum (Exeter), Calleva

Atrebatum (Silchester), and Corinium Dobunnorum
(Cirencester) belong, as well as the large *basilica* in the
last-named centre. Camulodunum (Colchester) and
Verulamium (St Albans) were rising anew out of the ashes
of the Boudiccan revolt. At Verulamium the great monumental *forum* and *basilica* are dated to the second half of
the year 79 by an inscription of Agricola, erected at the
very moment to which Tacitus ascribes his policy of
urbanization. The colonnaded timber shops destroyed by
Boudicca had also been rebuilt on the old messuages to
continue their earlier trading activities, while a new
market-hall and temple of native type had been erected.
The inhabitants of the hill-fort capital of the Durotriges
moved on to the Roman trunk road at Durnonovaria
(Dorchester), thereafter one of the two capitals of the
tribe. Two new *coloniae* for veterans were soon founded,
at Lindum (Lincoln) and at Glevum (Gloucester), while
at Aquae Sulis (Bath) the curative hot springs appear to
have received their first stone buildings. The native
aristocracy was in the best position to profit by the settled
peace and evidently could now afford to consider the
development of public amenities.

On the official governmental side it is instructive to
compare the new *coloniae* of Lindum (Lincoln) and
Glevum (Gloucester) with the new Camulodunum. The
last covered within its walls 108 acres and its chess-
board street-plan was laid out in Nero's later years. The
temple of Claudius, of which the great vaulted platform
was fireproof and indestructible, occupied its old position.
The town was as big as Roman Cologne, the *colonia
Agrippinensis* which was intended not only for Roman
veterans but for native inhabitants as well. Lindum and
Glevum, on the other hand, each covered just over forty
acres. Lincoln was for veterans of the Ninth Legion,

Gloucester for those of the Second Augusta. It is possible that Camulodunum, the *colonia Victricensis*, was for veterans from both legions called Victrix, the Fourteenth and Twentieth, and this might account for its double size. But on the Lincoln scale there is still room for other classes of inhabitant, though nothing is known of the size of the veteran drafts. Lincoln and Gloucester compare closely with African Thamugadi (Timgad), a small, purely Roman unit carved out of native territory, whose town-plan and buildings were ostentatiously and deliberately Roman in all their features. At Lincoln the spade has shown that the *colonia* occupied the evacuated fortress of the Ninth Legion: at Gloucester the final verdict on an apparently similar succession is awaited. The lands of both communities were certainly the older legionary *territoria*, once taken from the allied tribes, the Coritani in Lincolnshire and the Dobunni of the Cotswolds. But they are terrain which would be useless until Roman enterprise drained and developed it. Their loss might thus ultimately be envied but could not be immediately regarded as a hardship. The Romans had duly noted the feelings aroused by harsh expropriations at Camulodunum, and now avoided new confiscations.

Different from any of the towns hitherto considered was Londinium (London). Nature here contained the tidal Thames within hard gravel banks and made possible the construction of a bridge, where land traffic and sea traffic for the whole island met. The roads radiated from the bridge head, the sea lanes converged upon it from the Rhine, the Gallic coastal ports, and the North Sea, or by the Channel route from Bordeaux, Spain, and the Mediterranean. No question of status could prevent Londinium from becoming the natural centre for British trade and administration once the Roman engineer had picked it. If the first intention was to govern the province from Camulodunum, it is clear that within a generation the financial administration was using Londinium as its headquarters; while in the fourth century A.D. it was not only the seat of the provincial treasury but the residence of the civil governor who presided over the four divisions into which the province was then broken. In A.D. 100, if not before, the town was garrisoned like a provincial capital, and it seems certain that, whatever Camulodunum had been, the supremacy had by then passed to Londinium. It is London that furnishes mercantile documents on wooden tablets, a large city-hall for judicial and commercial business, fine imported artistic works in bronze and marble, and evidence of Romanization upon a scale matched in no other town in Roman Britain. It grew steadily, and when its walls were built, not before the third century A.D., they enclosed an area of 325 acres, larger than most Roman cities north of the Alps. As a trading centre the place was already well known when it was reduced to ashes during the rebellion of A.D. 60. During the following generation it was growing rapidly, like a boom town, and was ravaged by a great fire, dated to the twenties of the second century A.D., only to emerge phoenix-like from its ashes. Many of its buildings were no doubt half-timbered and the fire-fighting appliances of the Roman world were helpless against major conflagrations.

The Hadrianic fire of London coincided with a new outburst of building activity in the Romano-British towns. No doubt this represents the reaction of a generation yet more conscious of civilization and its meaning than the second generation after the conquest. Many towns in Gaul had taken even longer in the process of self-Romanization. But there can be no doubt also that the visit of Hadrian to the province, where he is recorded to have 'set much in order,' had in the civil area an effect no less powerful than on the northern frontier. The two scenes, military and civil, form one act. The most striking testimony comes from Viroconium (Wroxeter) on the Severn, capital of the Cornovii, where the great inscription, dedicating the city-hall and market-square of the town to Hadrian in A.D. 129–30, still wins the admiration evoked by all Roman monumental lettering. With this great building is contemporary the planned street-system, dividing at least 180 acres into spacious rectangular building-blocks, many of which were occupied by the large residences of tribal magnates. When these facts are considered in relation to the territory of the Cornovii, garrisoned in part and in due time producing a named auxiliary regiment, the town is seen as a defended centre for the wealth and enterprise of the tribal magnates. Such a centre was not the crowded and pulsating town of the Mediterranean world, of which country-life was as it were a centrifugal manifestation. It was rather the product of a centripetal movement, representing the creation by the countryside of a centre for its security. But, although these were very different things, the outward material effects had something in common, which Italian and British landowners might have shared with mutual comprehension.

Another town in which social requirements were developing was Ratae Coritanorum (Leicester), capital of the tribe out of whose territory the *colonia* at Lindum (Lincoln) had been carved. Under Hadrian the Fosse Way, approaching the town from Lincoln, was remodelled and fitted with milestones, no doubt at the expense of the Coritani both in money and compulsory labour. In the town itself a fine suite of public baths was also being built, with a public hall attached. By one of those mischances which are so vividly described by Pliny in the province of Bithynia, the line for the aqueduct feeding the establishment was miscalculated, and water seems thereafter to have been supplied from the adjacent river to a hand-filled cistern: work for municipal labour, but hardly consonant with the best standards of the day. It will suggest that the baths were by no means in continual use, and may serve to qualify a rosy view of universally extended social amenities frequently enjoyed.

The clearest picture, however, of the impulse started in the Hadrianic age is supplied at Verulamium (St Albans), where the town was entirely rebuilt, partly on and partly off the old site. The Flavian town, of trapezoidal plan, was replaced by a new oval town roughly twice as large, with two triumphal arches, of the twin type seen at Saintes and Langres, and a small theatre, convertible for shows as well as acting. Other public buildings no doubt await discovery, but the balanced excavation sampled in addition a residential quarter, in which there was a fair sprinkling of wealthy citizens' houses. These were comfortable dwellings, in many cases half-timbered and mostly a single storey in height, sprawling alongside or round a roomy garden-court. They are emphatically the country dwelling brought to town, and there is no sense of crowding or of the tight-lined planning that goes with urban development. Those who planned the town were determined that the gentry should have room. The shop-keepers, whose long narrow buildings jostled one another on the main streets, belonged to a different class, whose policy was minimum capital expenditure combined with maximum profit upon an outlay involving much higher risk than a modern manufacturer or retailer would care to face. A great defensive bank and huge dry ditch surrounded the whole town, with four main gates, and several posterns. As also at Corinium (Cirencester), the gates are of monumental type, built in masonry and planned with double carriageways and footways between semicircular towers, and they emphasize that such defences, while securing the town by night and shielding it against brigands or revolts, also reflected the pride of a tribal centre in its status. What that status was, as expressed in Roman constitutional terms, is uncertain. If a *municipium*, or chartered town, then it formed a special enclave within the tribal area, unless that area was formally attributed to it. There is no certain evidence for either arrangement, and it may well be that the towns remained unchartered townships, or *oppida*, whose status was defined in the treaty governing the tribal relations with the provincial government. Verulamium, however, is once described by Tacitus as a *municipium*, in a context which suggests that he is not using the word loosely but in its strict legal sense.

The relationship of tribal aristocracy to trade and to incoming settlers from elsewhere in the Roman Empire is obscure and difficult to determine. In other regions of the Roman world landowning and trading often went together, in the sense that a landowner would invest spare capital in a business run by his slaves. But intelligent business-trained slaves in the hands of Roman citizens, as the wealthy members of the tribal council soon became by serving in magistracies, graduated into freedmen, whose enterprise and ambitions all lay in the direction of trade. How many of these did a Romano-British tribal capital contain? No answer is at present possible, just as no estimate can be made of the number of Roman citizens in the form of retired soldiers or traders who settled there for business. Such folk undoubtedly existed. There was a 'guild of non-Roman citizens settled at Calleva' (Silchester), tribal capital of the Atrebates, which was the hub of the Roman road system to the west and south-west from London. How did these link with the Tammonii, one of the old families of the tribe, worshippers of Hercules Segomo? What, again, was the relationship between the tribal aristocracy of Venta Silurum (Caerwent) and Nonius Romanus, who was important enough to be excused his guild obligations and signalized his gratitude by a dedication to a native Mars Ocelus, whom he equated with Lenus, the god of his native Moselle? Such questions cannot be answered, but the fact that they can be put demonstrates the variety of the social scene and the many problems which a dearth of documentation leaves unanswered.

There is, however, another social problem upon which the scale and disposition of the tribal capitals gives some answer. Certain tribal capitals in Britain are exceptionally small. Two of them, Venta Silurum (Caerwent) and Venta Icenorum (Caister-by-Norwich), belonged to tribes whose resistance to Rome had been fierce and in the former case protracted. The Iceni had begun relations with Rome as an allied client-kingdom, whose royal family and restive nobility instigated a wild revolt when the kingdom was annexed. The wasting which followed crippled the tribal resources, so that Venta developed as a town, somewhat larger than its ultimate thirty-five acres, only in the second century A.D. At Venta Silurum the tribe perhaps lost less by stubborn resistance than the Iceni lost by rebellion. At all events town-life began sooner and, although the town never grew beyond its forty-five acres and always remained unpretentious, the place reflects on smaller scale what was happening elsewhere. By the early third century A.D. it was erecting an hono-

rary statue to a benefactor in regular Roman fashion.
One tribe had no central capital. The Durotriges of
Dorset, whose initial resistance to Rome had to be broken
by the storming of numerous hill-forts – the Life of Vespasian mentions twenty in Wessex – were divided between two centres, at Durnonovaria (Dorchester) and
Lindinae (Ilchester). This may have been due to the
separation of the two areas by the Blackmore Forest
(Alauna silva), just as in Gaul the Vocontii of the Vau-
cluse were governed from different centres in their two
main valleys. But the cleavage of a tribal area is for
Britain so exceptional that it is more easily regarded as an
early arrangement intended to break the unity of the
tribe and perhaps to facilitate its inclusion within the
client kingdom of Cogidumnus.

Uniformity, however, was no Roman constitutional
fetish. Indeed, nothing is more characteristic of Roman
imperial development than a readiness to work within
existing arrangements provided these could be assimilated
to Roman form. The history of the northern tribes of
Britain is an object-lesson in the handling of this principle.
Those permanently included within the province were
two, the far-flung Brigantes, whose lands extended from
sea to sea; and the Parisi, possessors of eastern Yorkshire,
thickly populated from of old. The Parisi had welcomed
Roman merchants for a generation before they became
part of the province in A.D. 71; and it was through their
territory that the army of Cerealis carried out its main
advance upon the Brigantes. That this move was peace-
fully received, if not welcomed, is shown by the subsequent immunity of the tribe from permanent Roman
garrisons, of which only one lasted, stationed at Derventio (Malton), the north-western gate over against the
Brigantes. Derventio always remained a garrisoned

centre, and was much used later for the collection of grain for the army. It may also have represented a standing insurance against an outburst of animosity between tribes. But the Humber crossing at Brough (Petuaria) was garrisoned until the early second century, and only then became the seat of the tribal capital, still described in the middle of the second century A.D. as a *vicus*, or village-community. The significance of this appears in its name, which in Old British means 'fourth'. There were thus at least four such centres within the tribe, a development closely comparable with that described by Strabo as obtaining among the allied Gallic tribe of the Allobroges. They lived, he states, 'in village communities', and adds that the village which was their governing centre had been embellished so as to become a city. The comparison is illuminating, the more so since Petuaria grew into existence, like some townships of Roman Germany, out of the village outside a fort. The inscription which mentions the *vicus* of Petuaria records the erection of a theatre-stage by an *aedilis*, or junior principal magistrate, and this implies some degree of civility. But the place never grew into a town. Another aspect of the picture is afforded by the tribal countryside. The houses of farming estates on the Yorkshire wolds early became Roman in build but their owners mainly eschewed all Roman amenities until the third century A.D., preferring the ways of their forefathers consolidated, as it were, but little moderated. Here, then, is an area where Romanization came late precisely because the inhabitants, using their freedom of choice, had held aloof from the brave new world.

The wider area of the Brigantes offers potentially and exhibits in reality wider variation. At York itself, under the shadow of the legionary fortress, there grew up first a large trading settlement outside the ramparts, and then, across the river to south-west, a still larger mart. This grew by the third century into a corporate town which by A.D. 237 had received the status of a *colonia* and had become the capital of the new province of *Britannia inferior*. The rich plain of York, which the legionary fortress dominated in the same way as Isca Silurum (Caerleon) oversaw the Glamorgan sea-plain, was the fattest region of the tribe. Here lay its fifty-five-acre capital, Isurium Brigantum (Aldborough), at the crossing of the Ure. Here too an increasing number of farming estates has been recognized, the homes of the tribal aristocracy. But there are many thickly populated areas where this villa-life has not yet appeared, and where town-life is either modest or non-existent. Neither Craven nor Cleveland, both heavily exploited agricultural districts, has yet afforded such manifestations. Calderdale, productive of inscriptions suggesting veteran land-settlements, seems without an urban centre. The Cumbrian sea-plain, boasting at Luguvalium (Carlisle) a town of some size and pretensions, has yielded no villa, though densely studded with native farms. The Durham magnesian limestone plateau so far exhibits one villa only, but no town. These widely separated districts do not, however, comprise the whole territory. The Pennines and their passes, all Lancashire and Westmorland, most of Cumberland, and most of Derbyshire (if it belonged to the Brigantes at all), present a picture of lands under military occupation, policed and patrolled by permanently stationed garrisons. There the native communities of fell and forest, tied to their flocks and herds, were kept from internecine strife and it seems that their little farms grew and spread. But neither the habit of life nor the economic level of such folk was conducive to an adoption of Roman ways. Their market needs were few and could be met either at tribal fairs or in the settlements for entertainment and trading which grew up round all but the wildest forts. So over a wide area of Brigantian territory martial law or its shadow reigned and the *pax Romana* spelt an unexciting daily life, punctuated by many duties to both tribal and central government. For the rest the pattern of the civilian areas is certainly uneven, if not always now to be descried; and it emphasizes the lack of unity and political cohesion which had originally brought upon the tribe the yoke of Roman rule. For people in this stage of development the yoke was heavy and the burden not light.

The military *vicus*, or village which grew up outside a fort, had, however, an important part to play in the economic development of northern Britain. It formed the centre for a local market as well as ministering to the recreation of the soldiers, and its development might be so promising as to tempt the serving soldier into business and eventual retirement. Most of its buildings are long narrow shops or taverns with an open front shut with sliding doors, and a large back room for goods or service. The proprietor and his family lived upon an upper floor. With the institution of land settlements for serving soldiers in the third century A.D. these extramural settlements became more than ever the local centres. Some were very large and most had corporate existence, a body of *vicani* governed by *magistri*. On or near Hadrian's Wall the *vici* at Chesters, Chesterholm, and Housesteads were larger than the fort. The Housesteads *vicus* was associated in the fourth century A.D. with a special gateway by which trade passed through the Wall to and from the territory beyond. The wide development of the *vicus* at the military supply depot at Corbridge made of it a virtual town. Air-

Figure 7

photography at Piercebridge (Co. Durham) or Old
Carlisle (Cumberland) and past field-observation at Old
Penrith (Cumberland) attest very large settlements there,
where a military road-centre supplied the traffic-routes to
a market. The substantial shops and taverns excavated in
the nineteenth century at Binchester (Co. Durham) witness a similar development for the same reasons. In Upper
Germany, as the frontier line advanced, not a few such
settlements were left without garrisons and, far from fad-
ing out of existence, continued to grow into prosperous
towns. In Britain examples of this phenomenon occur at
Luguvalium (Carlisle) and Caturactonium (Catterick
Bridge, Yorkshire). There are, on the other hand, many

places where this development never occurred. It did not happen either in Wales, except perhaps at Caermarthen, or in most lands west of the Pennines. It is significant that the places where it occurred remained important traffic centres, related to good agricultural land.

The tribes further north, in Lowland Scotland, now within the province and now outside it, were in the former event wholly subjected to military control. A difference of treatment is discernible. The Votadini, whose territory included Northumberland and Midlothian, were treated in far more friendly fashion than their neighbours the Selgovae, the one territory exhibiting few garrisons while the other is thickly studded. A similar discrimination was probably exercised between the Damnonii and the Novantae, as yet less easy to define. Control certainly extended to native settlements: the Votadini were permitted still to dwell in their hill-top town on Traprain Law, but the major hill-forts of the Selgovae show no such licence; Ruberslaw and the North Eildon stood empty and were occupied by Roman signal-stations. This pattern of control had already been exemplified among the hill-folk of Wales and the Pennines. Many of the Welsh hill-forts are known to have been emptied of their inhabitants and rendered useless for defence. There remained, reduced to helplessness, only the farming communities which the forts had dominated. The Brigantian hill-forts met the same fate: indeed, the action of destroying these north-British strongholds became, like the destruction of Moorish kraals, a by-word for military activity – '*dirue Maurorum attegias, castella Brigantum*'. In such areas, as on the Westmorland fells, Roman rule brought peace but hardly plenty. Yet it is well to recall that within any tribal area, however civilized the chief town and its notables or their country seats, there were many small farmers among whom the scale of prosperity, varying in some degree according to their occupation, never rose high. The small farmers or crofters provided rents and taxes for tribe and provincial government. Their lads must from time to time have had to face the conscription officer, seeking his periodical quota of army recruits. This background of toil and hard living is not wholly black, but its tones are always sombre. They throw the higher achievements into brighter relief, while emphasizing the fact that ancient polite society was not broadly based.

The foregoing review of the various British towns and cantons plainly shows that, as in Gaul, they were left to feel their own way towards a Romanization which proceeded wherever possible within native framework. It reveals also that the average British tribal notable cared more for his estates than for town-life. The great Italian landowners had sprung from the towns and made them their headquarters: and in addition to the country properties, their town-house was frequently closely related to shops or factories in which trades run by slaves and freedmen flourished. In this way wealth bred wealth. Contrariwise, the Romano-British landowner was based upon the country. For the most part the town was for him an occasional necessity rather than a permanent base of operations. But the creation of the towns does in fact show that some of the tribal gentry came to take the Roman attitude, establishing themselves in the town for at least part of the year and presumably keeping a profitable grip upon cantonal economics and local government. Tribal politics and family cliques or rivalries will have played their part in determining what proportion of the tribal aristocracy adopted these new habits. Again, those who owned the real property of new value, such as the clay-

land for tileries, the quarries for freestone and flagging,
the gravel for road-making, or the woods for timber, will
have been ready to profit by the new building programme. But the momentum was lacking to create a
sufficiently large steady market, except in such a centre
as London. The Romano-British towns thus tended to be
small. It is remarkable how many of them, upon receiving their walls or ramparts in the second century or
later, settled down at a size of round about 100 acres.
Some had unquestionably been larger. Calleva Atrebatum (Silchester) had begun ambitiously at twice the size,
Durovernum Cantiorum (Canterbury) had a large suburb
which was not included within fortifications. But Noviomagus Regnensium (Chichester), Venta Belgarum (Winchester), Ratae Coritanorum (Leicester), and Isca
Dumnoniorum (Exeter) all settled down at the 100-acre
size without sign of strain or constriction. Isurium Brigantum (Aldborough) was notably smaller. Only Corinium
Dobunnorum (Cirencester) remained exceptionally large,
at over 200 acres, a size which puts it into the class of
Verulamium (St Albans) and Viroconium Cornoviorum
(Wroxeter). All were the capital towns of early allies and
in such communities Romanization will have proceeded
at a rapid pace amid favoured treatment. All, too, were
set in fertile territory rich in cornland, pasture, and
timber.

The only town among them all to have been fully
excavated is Calleva Atrebatum (Silchester). But allow-
ance must be made for the fact that these excavations
were early, in many respects uncoordinated, and of very
uneven quality in execution. Yet the overall impression
may be taken as a substantially accurate picture of a
Romano-British town of the third and fourth centuries
A.D. It contained the administrative buildings and

market-place, four pagan temples and a small but central Christian church, public baths, a large *mansio* for the Imperial Post, and a fine extramural amphitheatre. The town-wall was an impressive structure, with a large fosse outside it and imposing semi-monumental gates. The main street was lined fairly thickly with shops and work-

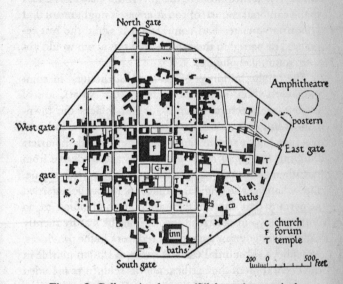

Figure 8. Calleva Atrebatum (Silchester); a typical Romano-British tribal capital

shops. There were about twenty-five really large houses and something like the same number of small ones, the former representing the houses of tribal notables, the latter the houses of administrators or merchants. To estimate accurately the population of such a place is difficult; surely at not less than 2,500 on the showing of the plan. But if, as seems very probable, many timber structures

were missed this number may have been doubled or
even trebled. On the medium reckoning, or even at
the highest, the town was, however, no more populous
than a small market town of today; and, when it is
considered how highly self-sufficing country folk of
the period contrived to be, this estimate may not seem
amiss. When the houses of the governing class are related
to the cantonal council of 100 *decuriones* it might mean that
about one-quarter had come to town while the rest remained dispersed in the canton, and this again would not
seem an unlikely figure.

The public buildings of Calleva (Silchester), in common with those of Venta Silurum (Caerwent), are of
modest architectural design. At both places the town-
hall (*basilica*) and market-place (*forum*) are combined
in a plan highly reminiscent of the legionary headquarters
building (*principia*) and thought perhaps to derive from
it. Others, however, have argued that the reverse is true.
But, whatever the original connexion, it may be regarded
as certain that the military architect had much to do
with the lay-out of British towns, since he was frequently
called in for government-sponsored work in the provinces.
At Calleva substantial use was made of Italian marble in
the decoration of the basilica, and its sculptures included
a large stone statue of the *genius*, *Tutela*, or guardian
deity of the canton, and a large bronze statue clad in
armour. The Baths of Calleva are again reminiscent of
military type, though as time went on they became less
so. In this specialized field of building technique an inter-
change of civilian and military architectural convention
is even more likely.

It has already been noted that the status of the cantonal
capitals is uncertain. But it may be regarded as sure that
the magistrates at least would become Roman citizens

upon entering office. This practice was founded upon a
very ancient political custom in the Roman world by
which allies of equally civilized status received the citizenship for their whole *ordo* of *decuriones*, while among
those of lesser cultural achievement the privilege was confined to holders of the higher magistracies. Nor need it be
doubted that upgrading will have taken place in communities becoming less backward. It must be remembered
that in A.D. 213 the citizenship was granted outright,
except in a limited number of specified classes, to all free-
born individuals within the Empire.

The executive officers who carried out the work of the
decuriones or *ordo splendidissimus*, as the cantonal senate
was called, were few in number. There were four principal magistrates, two senior, the *duoviri iuredicundo*, and
two junior, the *duoviri aediles*, all elected annually. The
senior pair were concerned with the administration of
justice on all civil cases below a certain value and minor
criminal cases. Civil cases of high value and criminal
cases involving capital punishment went to the Roman
governor's courts or to his juridical deputy, the *legatus
iuridicus*, which were held at the assize centres (*conventus*),
of which the location in Britain is unknown. All cases between Roman citizens went to Roman courts as a matter
of course. The junior pair were concerned with the letting
of contracts, the upkeep and repair of public buildings, or
installations. Both sets of magistrates celebrated their
election to office by games, entertainments, or gifts to the
community in the Roman manner; an *aedilis* is seen pre-
senting a new stage-front to the local theatre at Petuaria
(Brough on Humber).

On the fiscal side the *decuriones* were legally responsible for the collection of the Roman provincial taxation
in money and kind. They also determined and collected

such local taxation as the tribal council saw fit to levy. They were not initially responsible, however, for the assessment of the Roman taxes, which comprised a land-tax (*tributum soli*) and a poll-tax (*tributum capitis*). These were carried out by the Roman *censitores*, or census officers, and involved the compilation of a detailed list of populace, property, produce, and animals, upon which the initial taxation was based. The first census and subsequent general revisions were carried out by a senatorial special commissioner, of high reputation and probity. But the intermediate adjustments, rendered necessary by transfers of property, were carried out every five years by the tribal authority. For that occasion the two senior magistrates were chosen with especial care and received the title *duoviri quinquennales*, an honour valued for its indication of public trust and esteem. The revisions thus carried out would be agreed with the department of the procurator, the Imperial officer of equestrian standing stationed in London, who was responsible for the collection of the provincial taxes.

The money taxes were paid into the Imperial Treasury. The taxes in kind were delivered to the Imperial services for which they were levied. The corn-tax, for example, was mostly paid to the army authorities, and the *civitas* responsible for payment had to deliver it at the point indicated by them. Such a collecting depot was established during the first fifty years of the province at Rutupiae (Richborough), whence supplies were shipped northwards for campaigns. But Tacitus also speaks of long and awkward deliveries, which implies direct servicing of permanent garrisons as well. The financial and physical responsibility for the task fell upon the canton concerned.

The upkeep of cantonal roads concerned the community also, and for such main roads as were laid out and engineered by the central government the canton was required to provide materials and labour-gangs, who would work under supervision of the Roman military engineers. These roads comprised not only the trunk roads necessary for provincial communication and strategy, but the secondary roads which opened up the territory of the canton and linked its minor administrative centres. Anyone who sees the Roman south-west road streaking through the Wiltshire and Dorset downlands today, with its twenty-five-foot central causeway and the cleared belt defined by ditch and bank on either side of it, will get a grim idea of the work which the *civitates* had to perform. Even today the remains strike the eye almost as forcibly as a railway track. In addition to the construction and maintenance of the principal roads to the pattern and satisfaction of the central authorities, there was the upkeep of the Imperial Post. This elaborate service of courier-gigs, coaches, and heavy wagons was established for the use of Imperial officials. It was not, like the modern Postal service, a government institution run for the benefit of the public, but a service operated at public expense for the use of the government. The roads on which such a service ran were limited: the Antonine Itinerary, a document of the early third century A.D., with later alterations, gives a list for the whole Empire, in which Britain has sixteen routes thus equipped. Radiating from London, they serve all the cantonal capitals and cover the principal lines of penetration in the military areas. They are not always the most direct routes but they represent the principal traffic lines and are arranged in relation to the two principal fiscal centres of the time in the island, namely, London and York. As the work indicates, with differentiation, the roads were provided at about twelve-mile stages (those of the military districts are longer) with changing-stations (*mutationes*), where horses could be changed, and rest-houses (*mansiones*), where accommodation for the night was provided. The communities were expected to furnish and feed sufficient horses for the traffic – requisitioning might be resorted to in case of failure – and to keep the rest-houses in good order, furnishing them with fuel and the bare necessities of food. In the capital towns the rest-houses (*mansiones*) were large and commodious structures with bath-house attached. The upkeep of all these installations and equipment and the general cost of maintenance of vehicles, represented a substantial burden which must have fallen very heavily upon the *civitates* through which a volume of traffic passed, for example, Verulamium (St Albans), Durovernum (Canterbury), or Calleva (Silchester).

Two sites or establishments connected with towns or settlements remain to be described, although neither was a normal town. These are the spas of Aquae Sulis (Bath) and Aquae Arnemetiae (Buxton). Aquae Sulis, whose presiding deity was Sulis Minerva, was a small town, of about twenty-two acres, and its defensive wall, built in later Roman days, embodied in its masonry many tombstones of earlier inhabitants. But all structures inside the walls seem to have been dwarfed by the great curative Baths, the largest of their kind known in western Europe. The establishment as now visible seems to have been designed originally as three great swimming-baths or plunge-baths arranged in series, the largest, now the Great Bath, certainly at first uncovered and flanked by well-proportioned colonnades with alcoves. The water issues from a very deep and copious natural spring, at the high temperature of 120° Fahrenheit, and thus offers pleasant bathing apart from its curative properties, beneficial in cases of rheumatic and scrofulous complaints. If there also existed as part of the original concern hot baths of the everyday kind, dissociated from spas, their position is unknown. But these appear later at both ends of the building and exhibit many signs of repeated renewal and alteration. The Great Bath was also altered and improved by being roofed across by a great tunnel vault, with large open lunettes at each end, reminiscent of a railway station, from which the steam could escape. This huge vault, some thirty-five feet in span, demanded a massive strengthening of the portico piers, which were used to carry it, while the portico and its niches were converted by cross-ribbed arches into veritable flying buttresses, bringing the stresses down to earth. The highly ambitious and luxurious architectural scheme, which brought to Britain an example of thoroughly experienced Roman architecture, is shortly to receive the attention which it deserves.

No less notable are the architectural details. The outstanding pieces are the pediment and associated columns, capitals and entablature belonging to the temple of Sulis Minerva. The pediment, with a remarkable shield supported by flying Victories, is mentioned elsewhere (p. 108). But it may be stressed here that the capitals and entablature rank with the best sculpture of the Three Gauls and remind us that sculptors from the Chartres district were at work in Bath. The façade of the Four Seasons, dedicated by officials of a guild, is a conventional piece of architectural panelling, but the figured panels are endowed with both grace and vigour. There are also seen some notable decorated mouldings from a free-standing monument with four niches set back to back in pairs; while the coping designed as a mastiff biting a stag is one of those pieces of provincial art in which

Roman and medieval craftsmen seem to clasp hands across the Dark Age which divided them. It is not the only piece of its kind at Bath. There is an oddly medieval air about the pewter stag which serves as a candelabrum. Less anticipatory but no less curious is the large pewter mask or metope figuring a deity with painted beard and moustache and native style of hair-dressing: this is an old god of sea and water, comparable with the occupant of the great pedimental shield, Manwydd or his like, of whom Sulis Minerva, the goddess of the sacred spring, was presumably a daughter. Sulis Minerva herself is represented by a famous bronze head, commented upon elsewhere in this chapter (p. 108). The Roman spa at Bath is, in short, not only remarkable among the architectural remains of Roman Britain, but more than holds its own in comparison with other curative establishments in the Roman world, as is evident from known plans. The Romans themselves were not, however, interested in this point: for them the most notable thing about these 'richly adorned baths' was the curious fuel used upon the altars of the goddess, 'which did not waste away but turned to stony lumps'. This was the Somersetshire coal, a freakish fuel to Roman experience in general, though in fact coal was much used in Roman Britain (see p. 159).

In contrast with the notable relics and substantial information available concerning Aquae Sulis, the Buxton waters, Aquae Arnemetiae, afford all too little evidence of their Roman use. There is a reliable statement that lead-lined baths, associated with Roman structures, were seen in the late seventeenth century and further remains in 1780, all close to St Anne's well. St Anne herself may, indeed, well be the Christian version of Arnemetia, the patron goddess of the spring in Roman days, whose name is Celtic and means 'She who dwelt over against the sacred grove'. For the rest, the site had been, like Bath, in Roman military occupation during its earliest days, when its tepid waters were no doubt first observed. But, unlike Bath, it always remained on the fringe of the military area. In this it resembles such places as Wiesbaden (Aquae Mattiacorum) or Badenweiler, which lay close behind the military zone of Roman Germany, and attracted a numerous public of both soldiers and civilians. The social pleasures of such spas counted for at least as much as their curative qualities, and they were pleasant resorts for soldiers or officials on leave or for civilians on holiday.

The smaller centres within tribal territories have already been mentioned in connexion with the great roads. From the tribal point of view the most important were those which perpetuated the ancient organization of the territory. Celtic tribes were divided, for purposes of local government and for the raising of warrior bands, into *pagi* or *curiae*; and in some Continental tribes the *pagus* was retained as a basis for army recruitment in the service of Rome. Whatever its title, however, the local unit of territory, with its local magistrates, performed on a smaller and still more limited scale the functions of the tribal magistrates in the cantonal capital. Such units too, were of importance in fiscal organization, particularly in relation to the collection of taxes in kind; and this explains the interest of the Roman government in seeing that they were linked by the main road system. The little that is known about the internal arrangement of such townships is due to air-photography. It is clear that they were loosely planned, usually bellying out irregularly from the main road that passed through them. Accordingly, the plan of their walls is seldom regular: Kenchester is an irregular hexagon, Chesterton an ovoid, Alchester and

Dorchester (Oxon.) are sub-rectangular. But Alchester contained something like a little *forum*, if it was not a temple-precinct: Kenchester possessed a fine bath building and some houses embellished with sumptuous patterned mosaic pavements. All possessed numerous shops and workshops, indicative of their importance as local market centres; and these conformed to the normal type with narrow frontage and much depth and an upper storey for the proprietor's dwelling. Some towns were the stations of Imperial officials: Dorchester (Oxon.), in the Thames corn-lands, housed a *beneficiarius*, a military officer seconded to supervise road and river traffic or tax-collecting or both; at Irchester, amid rich horse-pastures, was quartered a *strator*, or remount officer. Facts of this kind demonstrate collectively that these small places had their own part to play in the administration of the canton and in the wider ramifications of Imperial taxation, but their remains are for the most part eloquent of modern neglect rather than ancient history.

It follows, however, that, for the sake of ensuring the safe-keeping of the administrative and local taxation-records or stores contained within these small places, the provincial government saw to it that such centres were walled. Examples of the kind are the Oxfordshire centres of Alchester and Dorchester, the Northamptonshire Irchester, the Lincolnshire Horncastle and Caistor on the Wolds, Kenchester in Herefordshire, Chesterford in Essex, Caister by Yarmouth in Norfolk, Catterick and Norton in Yorkshire. Norton was a *pagus* centre of the Parisi, while Kenchester and Catterick lay on Imperial post-roads. Most of the examples here selected have been chosen for their connexion with by-roads, lest they should be confused with the posting-stations associated with arterial routes. Many post-stations, presumably the *mansiones*, were also walled; and some were local road-centres of such importance that they must be regarded as performing a double function. Good examples of this sort on the trunk roads are Rochester (Kent), Towcester (Northamptonshire), Baldock (Hertfordshire), Great Casterton (Rutland), Chesterton (Northamptonshire), Wall (Staffordshire), Mildenhall (Wiltshire), and Droitwich (Worcestershire). By contrast, there were important road-junctions where no settlement of any importance appears to have existed; Badbury in Dorset, Old Sarum in Wiltshire, and High Cross in Leicestershire are striking cases. Examples abound of walled posting-stations which can hardly be considered large enough to rank as *pagus*-centres, and there may be instanced Penkridge (Staffordshire), Mancetter (Leicestershire), Ancaster and Littleborough (Lincolnshire), Leintwardine (Herefordshire), and East Stoke (Nottinghamshire).

The provision of defensive walls for all these centres might seem to indicate that the province was unusually troubled by raiders or by outbursts of local unrest. But in the Roman Empire this emphasis upon fortification of critical points was normal. In the absence of an effectively co-ordinated police force, it was important to ensure in advance that opportunities for brigandage or local peasant risings were eliminated by securing travellers' rests and local administrative or fiscal centres against them. That brigandage was in general effectively checked and restrained – its punishment by crucifixion or laceration by wild beasts was sufficiently severe – is attested by the open and carefree villa system obtaining all over the province. But prevention came before cure, and this explains conditions which look at first sight almost like a contradiction in terms.

The responsibilities of local government and increasing fiscal burdens tended in the later Empire to convert the decurionate, as membership of the tribal council was called, from an honour to an anxiety. But in the earlier Empire it was a prized distinction and an object of family ambition and rivalry. In Gaul, where such rivalry (*aemulatio*) laid the foundations of the French *émulation*, the effect was to run communities into heavy expenditure upon building programmes, financed both from public funds and private pockets. In Britain there must have been something of this, but it cannot be claimed as an outstanding feature of Romano-British town-life. This contrast is plainly due to a different attitude in Britain towards Romanization and its implications, and it has been held by notable authorities that it was based upon the relative poverty of British cantons as compared with the Gallic *civitates*. But, if the Gallic manifestation of public spirit was due to an outlook characteristic of the province, it should not be forgotten that Tacitus cited certain points of view native to Britain; and prominent among these, no less clearly persistent than *émulation*, was the habit of acquiescence in taxes and demands, so long as justice was observed. It may be asked what effect, as compared with Gaul, such an attitude may have had upon the relations between British landowners and their tenants, or upon cantonal taxation? If the exactions of the great Gallic landlords tended to provoke their tenantry to revolt and outlawry, British landlords were presumably held by public opinion to fairer conditions, which resulted in less wealth and therefore less opportunity or temptation to give way to family or cantonal rivalries. The moderating effect of such an attitude upon both cantonal building programmes and private munificence would produce a world which was more drab yet more kindly, and lives that were more humdrum yet more humane. It is perhaps, then, no accident that the difference in mode between the provincial characters matches the contrast in outward show. It may also well explain why in the second century, when taxation and exactions had not yet become a pressing public evil, the British landowners did not base themselves in large numbers upon the town as well as the country. Absentee landlordism did not suit the pockets of the majority.

The effect of this restrained indulgence in the attractions of town-life was neither everywhere the same nor constant. A striking case is provided by Verulamium, where a residential quarter, prosperous in the second century A.D., became ramshackle by the close of the third. Ploughing has removed later levels. This decline does not apply to the whole town and may represent not so much failing fortunes as curtailment by rural capitalists of the least binding of their obligations. When confidence was restored by the new government of Constantius Caesar, and opportunity by his presence in the province, not only did other residential quarters take on a new life, but considerable sums of cantonal or private money were spent on the erection, restoration, or enlargement of public buildings. The residential and public activity go together, for the spending of money upon contracts and materials attracted again to town those owners of real estate to whom the spending of money on public works meant profits. It should be remarked that all the known building on a grand scale is concerned with public amenities: the theatre is enlarged and embellished, the market-hall is rebuilt in new style, and the road between them is spanned by a triumphal arch. Politically, it no doubt implied a new programme of self-advertisement on the part of those who had not been prominent supporters of the recent usurper régime, and it might well represent new blood in cantonal politics and new opportunities in public life.

This notable revival of the showy side of town-life was itself soon subject to change. Three generations later the theatre was in complete decay and its fate was positively startling. The area in front of the stage was gradually buried many feet deep in tipped rubbish, high in vegetable content, containing many thousands of the insignificant coins of the last quarter of the fourth century A.D.; and such a deposit can hardly represent anything but the sweeping or periodic cleaning of trodden refuse from a market area, where large quantities of small change were continually passing. Thus, although Verulamium had lost its theatrical performances – and ascendant Christian feeling of the period would have deemed this gain rather than loss – it retained its importance as a market centre. But work on the late levels in the town houses, where these survive, shows that a flourishing life continued into the third decade of the fifth century A.D., when St Germanus was able to meet the notables of the town, in order to correct their heretical tendencies, and found them in a state of prosperity. The evidence thus comes into perspective. The residential quarter of the town had not in fact been decaying, and the town around them was not deserted. Its prosperity was concentrated in the shops and workshops which have in recent years been excavated. The environment of these, as the archaeology of any medieval city will show, might be squalid indeed, and the town none the less prosperous. There were still many lesser folk who found the town and, above all, its protective ring of walls, a source and condition of mercantile livelihood and profit. It is significant that the final activity

of which there is any trace is the provision of a piped
water-supply leading to the heart of the town.

This change in the character of the Romano-British
towns was not confined to the cantonal capitals. The
colonia of Lindum (Lincoln), founded at the close of the
first century A.D., had begun its existence as a chartered
town of privileged discharged soldiers, mostly legionaries.
Living in a small and rigidly planned town of some forty
acres, and initially supported by grants of money and of
land in the vicinity, they formed from the first a community attractive to traders and ready to invest in commercial enterprises. The town thus grew, and the growth
brought Lindum down-hill to the Witham and to the
associated canals between the Fens and the Trent. At this
peak of prosperity, as excavations have shown, the lower
town contained handsome and lavishly decorated buildings extending some distance behind the main street. But
in the fourth century A.D., by which time the lower town
had been walled in haste with re-used masonry and
tombstones, these buildings were totally dismantled and
their sites were occupied by modest non-monumental
structures honeycombed in turn by medieval cess-pits.
This decline in splendour would seem to imply that in
late-Roman Lincoln the same factors were operating as
in some cantonal capitals. The monumental buildings,
which had been the pride of its founders and their
successors, were destroyed, however this happened, and
submerged in a flood of traders' establishments, whether
shops or workshops.

Another town in which the decay of public buildings
did not spell an end to all prosperity was Viroconium
(Wroxeter). This place had originally grown up out of a
military trading settlement, to which had been transferred, at a date not yet established, the governing centre

of the Cornovii. It is by no means the only site in Britain
where a native capital came to occupy, presumably by
governmental ordinance, an erstwhile Roman military
site. Corinium Dobunnorum (Cirencester) and Isurium
Brigantum (Aldborough) are proved examples: Ratae
Coritanorum (Leicester) is almost certainly another; and
in every case the determining factor was certainly the
ready-made system of communications which the Roman
military engineer, employing troops and the tribal *corvée*,
had already provided. At Viroconium the ribbon-
development of traders' shops along the main road
created, as originally at Verulamium, the main street of
the town. Under Hadrian, in the years A.D. 129–30, there
was dedicated the large market-place and town-hall
of the enlarged town, over 180 acres in size. This town, of
which large areas are now known from air-photography,
is noteworthy for the substantial number of sumptuous
town-houses; and there can be no doubt of the fillip
which the visit of Hadrian to the province in A.D. 121
and his subsequent interest had given to Romanization
among the governing classes of the Cornovii. But later
days brought with them two successive blows to civic
pride. In the later second century A.D. the market-place
and town-hall were burnt down. In A.D. 296, when the
fortress at Chester was also destroyed, the same buildings were involved in a second fire and never again
reconstructed. Throughout the fourth century A.D. this
principal site lay derelict and occupied by booths and
workshop-shacks. Yet other amenities had not disappeared. Opposite the forum lay the town baths, a modest
but not incommodious suite, to which a hall-like building,
as at Ratae (Leicester), formed a social entrance-hall
or foyer. These baths lasted in good working order
until the eighties of the fourth century A.D., when the

military occupation of Chester came to an end and ceased to provide the necessary shield from Irish raids. During all this period, however, and even after the Baths in turn had been destroyed, the shops on the main street continued to function and prosper. In the end the wheel of fortune seems indeed to have come full circle and the town finished its existence as it began, by ribbon development of traders along the arterial road. More information is, however, needed as to the fate of the large houses. One, near the main street, continued to be occupied in fair order until the eighties. Here there may be seen an evident contrast with Verulamium. Viroconium lay in a garrisoned canton where raiding was evidently expected. The effect may well have been to drive the owners of estates into the shelter of the walled town. The result of such a policy would be to add to the trades population the cantonal magnates, whose estates would be run by bailiffs, taking the risk of raids but not offering as hostages to fortune the wealth or the attractive slaves of a well-appointed country house. As will appear below, when country estates are discussed, examples exist of country houses where something like a flight from the country might be thought to have taken place. At Isurium Brigantum this almost certainly happened. The large and wealthy houses have produced mosaic pavements, of which the style is not earlier than the fourth century A.D., while those in the north-west quarter of the town, which are reconstructed and late, are associated with fourth-century coins. It would seem, therefore, that the fourth-century town housed a substantial number of cantonal magnates.

Structural evidence concerning the quality of later-Roman social life in the extensively excavated towns of Calleva (Silchester) and Venta Silurum (Caerwent) is almost completely lacking. The excavators, reaping their harvest from the lower levels, paid little attention to the top layers, which afforded more fragmentary if no less precious evidence for the latest history of these towns. Although recent excavation at Caerwent has furnished evidence of late-fourth-century trading and manufacturing activity on the main street, the picture afforded is hardly large enough to form the basis for general inference. But both towns yielded so large a quantity of late-fourth-century coins, including copies based upon them or clipped coinage, and Silchester in particular so much late-fourth-century pottery, that there can be no doubt of a vigorous town-life in both places, whatever social elements composed it. At Venta Silurum (Caerwent), indeed, the buildings of the town had always been simple and unpretentious. Not only is the size of the place and the scale of its buildings small, but the principal houses, if provincial-Roman in plan, were most modestly equipped. Mosaic pavements and heated rooms were rare and bath-suites still rarer, 'Comfort without luxury' was the fashion of the Silures, possessing much upland territory and forest, not to mention their thirty years' initial hostility to Rome.

Another development, however, took place of which archaeology begins to afford a little evidence. As these communities became isolated in the fifth century A.D. and as the lands about them became less safe, they must have depended increasingly for their food-supply upon local harvests. At Verulamium a late phase in one of the large houses is represented by a corn-drying installation. A story has also survived of the timely relief of famine in sixth-century Isca Dumnoniorum (Exeter) by the arrival of a storm-driven corn-ship. It has been suggested with great likelihood that the Dark-Age system of dykes on the approaches to Calleva (Silchester) in fact indicates the limits of the lands upon which the food-supply of the town depended and which it was vital to conserve. Something of the same kind has been postulated for London and the similarity between the two systems is certainly close. If this interpretation be correct, Britain has yielded archaeological evidence of a stage in urban devolution rare indeed and precious to the historian.

As the picture of Romano-British urban civilization emerges, sometimes light and often dark, it becomes clear that the whole composition must have been flat and un-inspired when compared with the cities in southern Europe or even with many towns north of the Cevennes. There are, moreover, certain concrete particulars in which more than a general comparison can be made. Two very closely connected material achievements of Roman civilization are sewerage and water-supplies. It is certain that in Britain, as in Gaul, the majority of can-tonal capitals did not possess a general sewerage system. Sewers are entirely absent at Calleva (Silchester), where the baths, for example, have their own special outflow unconnected with any general scheme. Venta Silurum (Caerwent) and Venta Icenorum (Caister-by-Norwich) both exhibit the same deficiency, though all these towns had a chess-board plan of streets. Nor has chance excava-tion ever hinted at the existence of any system of the kind in other cantonal centres. But at Lindum (Lincoln), con-structed by Roman contractors for Roman ex-servicemen colonists, there is an elaborate system of main sewers with man-holes and feeders, which was laid down over an area somewhat larger than that of the *colonia* when walled. This brings Lindum into line with the principal cities of the Empire. No record exists of a similar system at Camulodunum (Colchester) or Glevum (Gloucester), which so closely resembles Lindum in other features: but this does not disprove its possible existence at either place.

Water supplies are better attested, but no example is known of the grandiose aqueducts which led distant springs to so many Roman towns. An obvious candidate for such a scheme would be Londinium (London). Lindum, however, boasted a very remarkable water-supply, forced up to the town from springs lying to the north-east through a rare type of water-main comprising tile pipes very heavily jacketed in concrete. There was at least one branch serving the extended town, but nothing is known of distributive methods. Several cantonal capitals, on the other hand, were served by a gravity supply carried below ground in timber pipes united by iron collars, which have appeared at Verulamium (St Albans), Corinium (Cirencester), Calleva (Silchester), Venta Silurum (Caerwent), and Venta Icenorum (Caister-by-Norwich). This type of conveyance was much favoured by military engineers, for the obvious reason that the pipe-line was hidden from sight below ground, and numerous examples of such systems are associated with Roman fortresses and forts in Britain, as in other frontier provinces. For urban use the disadvantage of such installations is the need for apparatus, such as buckets, pumps, or water-wheels, to raise the water to a convenient level after it has reached its terminal distribution-tank. Another type of supply is the open leet or water-course, of which an example nine miles long fed Durnonovaria (Dorchester, Dorset), while a duct of a similar kind seems to have been planned for Ratae (Leicester), but failed, as such projects sometimes did, owing to lack of skill in levelling. Such open conduits are also known to the military, and are matched on Hadrian's Wall at Aesica (Greatchesters). Only Viroconium

(Wroxeter) furnishes evidence for a supply reaching the town by a leet and serving not only lead and timber pipe-lines for private distribution but an overflow (*aqua caduca*) for a street-side duct, comparable with Hobson's Conduit in Cambridge. The Wroxeter duct was here and there tapped by sluices for flushing private latrines. The system is thus sufficiently developed to afford special supplies of both drinking-water and flushing-water to privileged folk. In this respect Viroconium is as far advanced as most Roman towns, where supplies were conceived as intended first for public fountains, then for baths, and only thereafter, as availability might dictate, for the private consumer.

In respect of its public water supplies, Britain thus compares not so ill with other frontier provinces, though it falls far short of the best Mediterranean standards. Other bases of comparison are hard to find, though artistic material provides highly interesting information. Here it may be remarked that, although the amount of Romano-British public art is small, its paucity must be related to the continuity of habitation and consequent destruction of Roman levels which is a feature of most of the important town-sites in Britain. Among surviving works, the bronze heads from life-sized statues of Claudius, originally from Camulodunum (Colchester), or of Hadrian, from Londinium (London), are not first-class works; but they are good examples of the class of statue commissioned by provincial centres, and hold their own with other provincial works of the kind. The York head in stone of Constantine, on the other hand, is a highly notable piece of work by any standard for its power and style: weathered though it is, it has not lost the freshness and virility of touch which is its outstanding characteristic. First among portraits of Constantine in date, it takes a first place among them for its dramatic force. Among cult-statues, Sulis Minerva from Bath, goddess of Aquae Sulis, is a positively attractive piece, with a firm classic restraint worthy of a Pre-Raphaelite studio. The shield-emblazoned pediment from her temple is a bold and original treatment of a hackneyed design which lifts it out of the commonplace into the realm of vigorous and sensitive art. From what is known of this public work and its quality, the province in its hey-day cannot be held lacking either in public taste or the means to gratify it, and its standards of taste cannot be dismissed as negligible. Recent discoveries of wall-paintings in Verulamium and Leicester have shown that private taste, even in comparatively modest houses, welcomed gay and elaborate patterns, though the colour schemes do not appeal to modern eyes.

CHAPTER THREE

THE COUNTRYSIDE

ROMAN villas are so well-established in Romano-British archaeology as to require, paradoxically, some explanation. Most have been recognized, and many rendered famous, through their mosaic pavements, which today would grace sumptuous country houses. But while country houses erected for pleasure existed in the Roman world, they were exclusively the privilege of the very wealthy. The late-Flavian villa at Fishbourne near Chichester is a remarkable example, worthy of a great official or the princely heirs of Cogidumnus. The normal Roman villa was not a liability but a profit-making farm, and the richest villas in Roman Britain conform to this economic basis. Comfortable on the average, luxurious at best, and squalid at worst, Romano-British villas ranged in size from cottage to mansion, and the associated acreage varied accordingly. Nor are they to be connected with Roman immigrants rather than native Britons. Roman settlers there were, retired soldiers, administrators, or even investors, but these were a minority compared with native British landowners, the principal farmers and notables of the tribes. The villas mostly represent the adoption of Roman standards in greater or lesser degree by natives of substance.

The first villas, like the towns, must have been, with due exceptions, simple and unpretentious; and three examples, two from the territory of the Catuvellauni and one from among the Belgae, will serve to illustrate the point. Park Street near St Albans and Lockleys near Welwyn began their existence as a single range of four or five rooms, divided by a passage from back to front. Park Street had a basement storehouse at one end, but neither building appears to have had a substantial upper storey. Catsgore (Somersetshire) is even simpler, comprising little more than a couple of detached barns, perhaps sub-divided in timber. In this it closely resembles the earliest Roman buildings at Langton (E. Yorks). But all three houses were erected on the site of earlier native huts, two of oblong plan at Park Street, and single round huts at Lockleys and Catsgore. Thus, however simple the new houses of Roman structure, there was a profound difference in solidity and comfort between them and the native buildings whose place they took, and the change doubtless represented considerable capital expenditure in the owners' eyes. As for standards, it is instructive to compare these plans with that of the smaller English farm-house of the seventeenth century. The types compare so closely that the known simple standards of the English example might illustrate those of earlier days. The important point is that Roman building fashions, though not yet Roman luxury, had been adopted within a generation of the conquest. The type recurs in the third century at Frocester (Gloucestershire).

The materials used in such houses were not necessarily the most solid and permanent. Stone foundations may connote half-timber superstructures rather than a building wholly of stone. At Ditchley (Oxfordshire), the timber posts which formed the first version of the earliest house plainly indicate the simplest kind of structural beginning, comparable with the now rare but once common timber arcades of Norman domestic architecture, of which carpentry made a delightful thing. The first stone-built Ditchley house differed little from Lockleys or Park Street, and it is probable that only a loft-like first floor

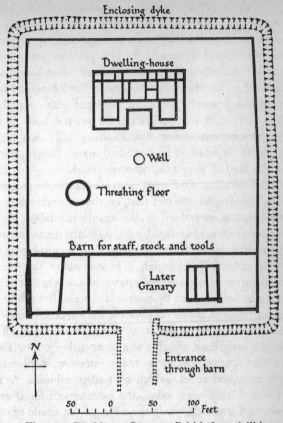

Figure 9. Ditchley, a Romano-British farm (*villa*)

was provided, if at all. But about the turn of the first
century A.D. there were added a new stone-built veranda
and projecting end rooms which gave to the establishment both privacy and a new elegance. There was now
room for recreation and entertainment in what had been
previously a workaday farm, wherein the whole house-

hold lived together. Socially speaking, the new plan
divided the household and accentuated the position of
master and mistress. In Britain this type of house became
widespread, and it brought the new province into touch
with the mainstream of contemporary West-European
domestic architecture. For in Gaul or the Rhineland the
design was generally common, and went with a sizeable
farm. And so it was in Britain, for on the basis of its
granary accommodation the Ditchley villa has been
related to an estate of five hundred acres. This supplies,
then, a kind of yardstick, however rough, by which the
size and standing of different kinds of villas can be gauged.
Even allowing for the fact that, on the ancient system of
crop-rotation, one-third of the arable lay fallow each
year, it becomes clear that by this standard the numerous
bigger villas must have been related to very substantial
estates indeed. Not enough is known about the social
organization of such larger estates to say whether they
were run by slaves or by crofter-labourers. But where a
resident staff of labourers appears, their accommodation
nearly always takes the form of a barn-dwelling, frequently ranged on one side of a farmyard or court. This
structure, convenient for so many purposes, is planned
with nave and aisles divided by timber columns. As in
Friesian farm-houses today, the nave served for stores,
tools, and livestock, while the aisles or the whole of one
end of the building were partitioned to house the workers.
In the form of a subsidiary building essential to the working of a farm this type of house was so general, even in the
largest establishments, that its prototype has been sought
in the pre-Roman days. But no proof of such antecedents
has yet appeared, and it may well be that the type is
borrowed from the Italian *villa rustica*. There are some
villas also in which this type of house is the only domestic

Tombstone of Thracian cavalry-man from Gloucester, riding down a western Briton: an episode of the early days of conquest. [p. 25]

Borcovicium (Housesteads) with Hadrian's Wall and military way, looking W. *Crown Copyright*. [p. 48]

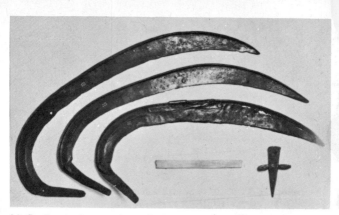

(*a*) Scythes and mower's anvil, from Newstead (Roxburghshire) for clearing land or trade. [p. 132]

(*b*) The Multangular tower, York, of *c*. A.D. 300: the neater masonry is Roman, the larger Plantagenet. [p. 61]

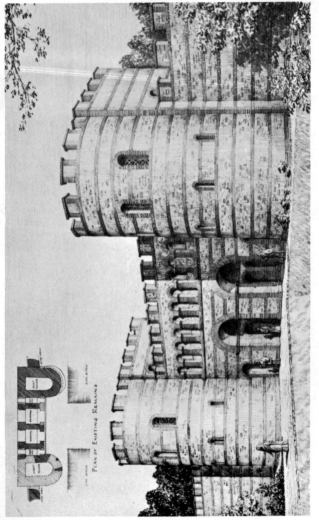

The London gate of Verulamium (restored). [p. 77]

4

Celtic fields, Smacam Down (Dorset). *Crown Copyright.* [p. 131]

5

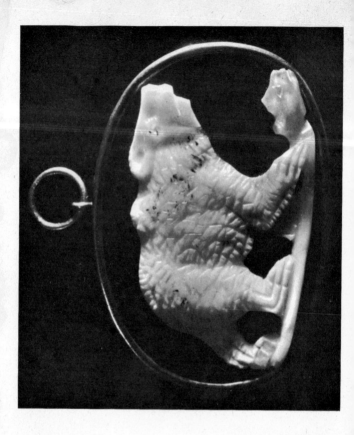

Cameo of a British bear, South
Shields (Co. Durham). [p. 162]

(a) Ladle handle, Capheaton (Northumberland), depicting an Empress, Mercury, god of trade, with a pack-man and shepherdess, the deities of corn and wine, sea and river – an epitome of British trade. [p. 198]

(b) Head of Claudius from Camulodunum, found in the River Alde (Suffolk) : a relic of religion, loyalty, and revolt. [p. 108]

7

Capital from Corinium (Cirencester), with Autumn and Winter, in north-west European style. [p. 190]

accommodation present, as for example Clanville (Hampshire) or Denton (Lincolnshire). These represent either small tenant farms or bailiff-run establishments, where the distinction between tenant or supervisor and workers was less sharply defined. Some, as at Castlefield (Hampshire), are so primitive in their arrangements that any distinction seems out of the question.

The planning of the houses so far described is determined by work. No mention has been made of bathhouses, because in the earlier Romano-British villas of this class they are a luxury rarely supplied. It is, indeed, one of the evidences of advancing civilization that in most later villas a bath-house, however simple, is an essential part of the plan. The next class of house on the upward scale, the so-called corridor house, is a development of the Park Street type of house, by adding to the number of rooms, and linking them with a front corridor. A bath-house was often attached to one end, or set closely adjacent to avoid the risk of fire. In such houses there is a tendency for the main rooms to lie at the end of the range, but a single large central room also tends to come into prominence. This is the dining-room, the social centre of Roman private life, bracketed by Tacitus with baths as the hallmark of civility; and it must be understood that in educated Roman circles the meal was savourless without good conversation and literary entertainment. A plan of this kind is accordingly the silent witness of the adoption of such standards by British well-to-do circles. But there are also corridor houses of which the planning is still more deliberately balanced, with rooms disposed in relation to garden or landscape. Such villas, as at Folkestone with its Channel view, are not necessarily very large, but they evoke a picture of yet another kind of sensibility.

The conversion of a corridor house into a courtyard house is dictated by size of household and estate rather than by other cultural or aesthetic considerations. The courtyard house always gives an impression of great size, and it is possible nowadays to exaggerate this, when so much that would now be arranged in storeys was in Roman Britain spread out upon the ground floor. Nevertheless, the biggest of these villas, as at Bignor, were large indeed, for the reason that in a society based upon slavery or small tenants, even moderately wealthy folk tended to accumulate large households. Britain has not furnished such scenes of daily life as grace the funeral monuments of the Moselle valley in lively variety. But there is no reason to think that the life of the wealthy in the provinces differed in its essentials. So the kitchen scenes of Gallia Belgica, with their cooks and scullions, the hunting scenes with grooms and estate lads, or the boudoir scenes with mistress and maids, might be applied to the world of the large Romano-British villas almost without observing the change of locality. What must be emphasized, however, as a social fact, upon which stress has already been laid, is that villas so large as Woodchester, where much remains unexplored, or Bignor, also with two courts, comprise both residential and workaday quarters. The inner garden court with its vast house, enormous central dining-room, and imported marble sculptures, is reached through an outer courtyard flanked by a pair of barn-dwellings of the type associated with farm-workers and farm-stock. The direct connexion of this richest of houses with the development of an estate is thus demonstrated by the plan.

Woodchester was uncovered and published in an age when evidence for the growth or evolution of villas was not sought. To perceive such a phenomenon it is neces-

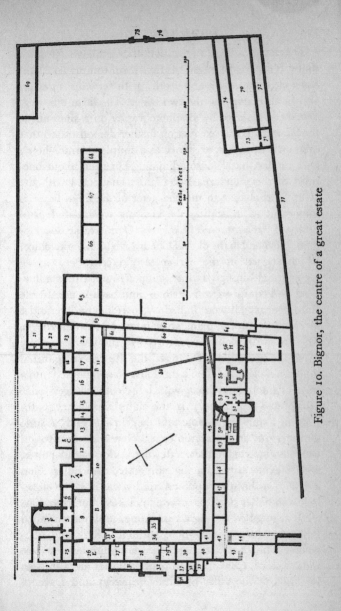

Figure 10. Bignor, the centre of a great estate

sary to go to a later excavation at Northleigh (Oxford-shire). This great house in its final form comprised a vast courtyard house of many rooms, with servants' quarters and baths occupying the two wings. The farm buildings have been descried by air-photography on a site outside the courtyard. But excavation further demonstrated that the house began its existence as a simple corridor-house with modest bath-house adjoining, covering about one-third of the later area but plainly connected with the farm. This change in the character of the main house is important as indicating the growing wealth and pros-perity of the estate and its owners. Comparable develop-ment is evident in the plan of Chedworth (Gloucestershire) which started in the earlier second century as three separate half-timbered wings grouped round a little valley-head and equipped with a stone-built bath-house. In the third century all were linked by corridors and verandas to form a unitary plan, with inner and outer courts. Maximum development occurred in the fourth century when the spring which watered the site was reorganized to feed a *nymphaeum*. The bath-house was converted into a suite of intense dry heat, with large cold plunges (once interpreted as a fullery). In the main house a new bath-suite of damp heat was established in one end, a large dining-room added at the other. New reception rooms were also inserted in the north wing. As for manufactures, recent exploration, having eliminated the fullery, has also shown that the supposed smithy was in fact a stoke-hole and boiler stand, from which massive iron cross-bars were dismantled during a rebuilding, itself discontinued in favour of a new stoke-hole, without boiler-stand, else-where. The bars, left derelict, were misinterpreted as smith's stock. Conversion to manufactories has also been surmised at the villas of Titsey (Surrey) and Darenth

(Kent), but in both the changes may well prove to be related to bath-suites. The process evident at Northleigh and Chedworth is matched in greater or lesser degree in many villas. There are few which did not grow in prosperity, even from small beginnings: and this is something to put beside the modest development of town life, which appears to blight the province and to stamp it as unfruitful.

Yet not all villas passed through the same kind of development. An instructive contrast is provided by Llantwit Major, in the Glamorganshire sea-plain. This estate developed in the second century A.D., administered from a simple courtyard house with modest farm-buildings attached, of which the most important was a barn-dwelling for the estate staff. At the beginning of the fourth century A.D. the main house was deserted, and fell into ruin. The barn-dwelling, on the other hand, functioned actively for another century; and it becomes evident that the estate continued to exist as an economic unit, but that its owners no longer dwelt there. Whether they had migrated behind town walls in times of uncertainty, or whether, for example, failure in the male line had transferred the estate to another family, cannot be revealed by the plan.

Normally the social picture implied by the planning of large villas is not unkindly. The master's house is flanked with quarters for servants or slaves which were not so sordid as to merit concealment. Nearly all, however, are associated with the practice of infant exposure, repellent to modern civilized folk, to a degree suggestive of a slave or serf population whose increase was harshly limited. This phenomenon is particularly marked at Hambleden (Buckinghamshire), where a small but comfortable farm overlooks an area honeycombed with successive corn-drying ovens in every variety of form, and flanked by simple barn-dwellings. The occupants of the house later reversed its main front, so that it now looked away from the work-yard, as if this had become too much of an eye-sore. It is tempting to recognize here a slave-run estab-lishment engaged in corn-production on a large scale and managed, whether for a rich proprietor or for the Imperial Government, by a prosperous freedman bailiff.

It would be difficult in the present state of knowledge to say where villa-life began to flourish on a wide-spread scale, but it may be recognized that in some dis-tricts its beginnings came much later than others. A remarkable case of a late start occurs in the territory of the Parisi in east Yorkshire. Here, at the excavated villas of Langton and Rudston, the agricultural ditches which mark the first phase in the history of the site are strewn with pottery belonging to the late first century A.D. In other words, they mark the new phase of activity in culti-vation stimulated by the *pax Romana* and by the demands of taxation or levies in kind made upon an allied com-munity by the Roman government. But the first modest buildings in the Roman manner at both sites do not come into existence until the third century A.D. This again marks the incorporation of the tribe within the newly constituted province of Britannia Inferior and the more insistent development of the natural resources within easy range of its new capital at York. But amenities can hardly be said to exist until the fourth century A.D., by which time the still greater insistence upon the develop-ment of local economy and the ever-growing tendency to levy taxation in kind rather than in money, caused a rise in values and prices of agricultural produce and increased the wealth of farming folk. The two villas could then be furnished with mosaic pavements and bath-houses, the latter of real luxury at Rudston. Vigorous local schools of mosaic workers, copying classical models with enthusiastic infidelity, grew up to meet the demand. A house of considerable architectural pretensions at Harpham belongs to this period, though its beginnings were earlier.

A second area where development came late is the north-east corner of the territory of the Brigantes, now County Durham. The villa at Old Durham has a bath-house which belongs to the fourth century A.D., and large threshing-floors of the same date. But the agricultural ditches which, as at Langton or Rudston, mark the earliest dated phase of activity on the site, yielded Antonine pottery. This is interesting because it marks a forward movement of Romanized property-holders in correspondence with the advance of the Roman frontier from the Tyne to the Forth.

There is no indication that the Old Durham site outlasted the severe troubles of A.D. 367–9, when Hadrian's Wall fell and was reorganized in a fashion so different from ever before. Open settlements so far north hardly seem to have been regarded as safe. But the villas of the Yorkshire Wolds lasted, behind their new coastal signal-stations and naval protection, until at least the opening of the fifth century A.D.: and the silver hoards of clipped *siliquae* which formed the money of account in the first decades of that century reach as far north as the Fylde and Tees. The peasant militia of Hadrian's Wall may have faded out as an effective frontier force, but the inner territory of the Brigantes was still intact and Roman, although the central government of the Empire was no longer in control of it. The same can be said of the coin evidence from Britain further south, and there is a very large number of villas which have produced coinage as late as the close of the fourth century A.D. The Somerset-

shire villas have long been cited as productive of a striking number of late-fourth-century silver coin-hoards; and
this special phenomenon has a special explanation related
to the silver-lead mines (p. 151). But the association of
late coinage with villas is not confined to Somersetshire
and is true of many sites south-east of a line drawn from
east Yorkshire to Devon.

This evidence may seem to disregard or contradict the
fact that a considerable number of sites cannot be shown
to have survived for so long. There are numerous villas,
widely dispersed, from which the recorded coins do not
go beyond the fifties and sixties of the fourth century A.D.;
and, while negative evidence of this kind may always lie
open to revision, there must be some substantial truth
behind this apparent termination of activity, as Haverfield long ago perceived. It must in fact have a connexion
with the troublous years which culminated in the invasions
of A.D. 367–9, when the province was beset on all sides by
raiders from overseas and much damage was done. It
would, however, be a mistake to exaggerate the permanent effect of these years of ill fortune. In east Yorkshire,
for example, the damage done at Langton was repaired
and an age of prosperous activity ensued. In Lincolnshire an entirely new villa at East Denton came into being after A.D. 369, and although it is of the barn-dwelling
type and therefore perhaps a bailiff-run farm rather than
an owner's residence, its creation nevertheless attests that
confidence in the peace and potential prosperity of the
countryside still reigned. At Great Casterton a villa in
open country was being actively reconstructed in the
eighties. It might be guessed that what caused the ultimate collapse of the villa system was not the insecurity of
the countryside so much as the collapse of the world upon
whose markets farming had depended.

No consideration of villas as a whole is complete without some reference to those mosaic pavements which have so often indicated their existence. The most famous and most evocative are those decorated with figure-scenes from mythology. But when an attempt is made to estimate the position of the patron in the choice of pattern, it must be borne in mind that the range of patterns available will have depended upon the pattern-book of the firm which laid the pavement. Again, the execution of the work might vary sharply according to the competence of the worker. A striking example of this is furnished by the Cirencester pavement of the Four Seasons, of which, out of three surviving, two are fashioned with sensitive grace while the third is a coarse and clumsy rendering of the same subject, wholly lacking in deftness of line or subtlety of colour-blending. Entire compositions, based upon original designs of obvious breadth or delicacy, could become mere caricatures in the hands of inexperienced or over-ambitious workmen. Such are the Wolf and Twins pavement from Aldborough, now at Kirkstall Museum, Leeds, the Venus pavement at Rudston (E. Yorks), and the Apollo and Marsyas pavement, from Lenthay Green, Sherborne (Dorset). A comparable failure in detail marred the Horkstow pavements, though in some reproductions of lost examples the copyist must bear his share of the blame. The fact that such standards of workmanship passed muster serves as a check upon the sensibility of Romano-British patrons. It is clear that many were about as far from an appreciation of classical taste as a worker of samplers from a designer of Gobelin tapestry. What is remarkable is that they should have wanted such things at all, particularly when a rich and attractive variety of conventional patterns in abstract design was also available, which native instinct might have prompted

them to choose. The choice then becomes something pur-
poseful, as deliberate as Chaucer's choice of classical
legend and interpreted in as crude an idiom. It becomes a
reflection, however pale, of classical culture.

There is no doubt, then, that the richer villa-owners
appreciated classical themes, and it is certain that many
of their choices were directly linked with classical habits
of mind or behaviour. The Dido pavement from Low
Ham need not mean that its owner was an enthusiast for
Vergil, but its existence does show that this was the idiom
of his choice; while the style of the design suggests that an
African workshop may have produced the pattern. The
Otford (Kent) wall-plaster, with its Vergilian scenes and
quotations, attests that same feeling in a kindred field.
No less striking are the dining-room pavements from
Aldborough and Lullingstone. In the former house, the
undecorated semicircular margin which, in the Roman
manner, held the three couches for diners, looked on to a
rich panel, now vanished, which formed a complemen-
tary centre-piece to the nine standing figures of the Muses
with Greek inscription. At Lullingstone a well-drawn
and spirited scene of Europa and the bull forms the
centre-piece and is embellished by a verse couplet which
has the amateurish ring of impromptu production at
the dining-table. These pavements and their planning
reflect good cheer and good company in the Roman style:
what was mannered in the first century A.D. had become
manners in the fourth.

Some pavements are even more positive in their reflection of exotic feeling. The Brading (Isle of Wight) pavements, with their scenes from Eleusinian legend, their
astrologer sage, and Abraxas, the Gnostic deity, must
represent not only a special order from a client, but a
specially concentrated line of taste. The Orpheus pave-

ments of Cirencester and the south-west are a Romano-British speciality and belong to a moment when the tale had become a vehicle of both pagan and Christian teaching. Dionysiac legend also had its place, as at East Coker (Somerset), where the story of the divine birth may be recognized. The Labours of Hercules appear at Bramdean (Hampshire), the story of Cyparissus at Leicester. These echo not Vergil, but the hardly less beloved Ovid. Genre scenes are less common, and this in itself suggests a fairly rigid adherence to the pattern-book rather than the commissioned composition. But the hunting-scenes from Pitney, unfortunately only fragmentary, or the combined chariot and horse race at Horkstow, the *bigae et equi desultorii* of Roman aristocratic sports, must represent the special commission, as plainly related to the particular tastes of the client as the Gnostic pavement at Brading.

A half-way stage between the purely conventional pattern and the figured pavement is represented by the marine compositions of sea-creatures, fish, and shell-fish, or by the heads of Neptune, commonly though not exclusively associated with baths. These also are based upon Mediterranean models, but the idea is one so easily borrowed that it would be unfair to dub them representative of Mediterranean taste. They stand rather for a specialized pattern applied to a particular type of activity, namely, bathing. The purely conventional pattern, on the other hand, is linked with no special room or purpose, and its ubiquity proclaims it as the prime favourite of Romano-British taste, with both patron and worker. There is no doubt that, as Sir Thomas Kendrick has observed, it ministered to the native British predilection both for abstract pattern and for that equality of emphasis upon pattern and background which gave them an almost magical interchangeability. There were, too, certain shapes, and notably the pelta, which had long been part of the repertory of Celtic art: and these were now employed, always with an eye to background, in new patterns of classical rigidity wherein colour played the major part. This was a new movement in British art, matched by the contemporary advances in enamel-work. As the vehicle of unity in design, colour now took the place of flow, and the desired effect, rarely unachieved, was of a glowing kaleidoscopic pattern controlled by its rigidity of form but softened by the fact that, while major patterns produced the over-all effect, the eye might dwell with equal satisfaction on minor designs within the major units. Further the colour scheme was seldom harsh or clashing: in contrast with the hot contrasts of Mediterranean marbles it reflects the cool days and soft colours of the British climate. The colours glow, but in rich restraint, as in a page of the Lindisfarne gospels.

Excavation at such villas as Park Street and Lockleys has revealed that Romanized buildings succeeded native farms of a primitive kind, composed of groups of rectangular or circular huts. But it is also a well-known fact that throughout the province many farms of this poorer sort retained their form little altered through the centuries and in general hardly affected by the Roman world around them. Evidence for this continuity of native habit abounds in large areas throughout the island: Salisbury Plain, the Dorset chalk-lands, parts of the North and South Downs, the Fenland, the Long Mynd, and Upper Wharfedale may be cited as typical regions of the kind. It would, however, be wrong to suppose that this ubiquity of native farms represents the existence of an anti-Roman movement or the presence of a populace reluctant to avail itself of better conditions: for excavation reveals that the inhabitants of such places were as Romanized as their means permitted them to be. Some other explanation of the state of affairs is therefore required, and the way thereto is cleared if it can be accepted that the Romanized villa and the native farm started from the same cultural level; for it then becomes necessary to suppose that the difference must lie in the social relationship of their occupants. The social framework of the Celtic tribe was explained by the Romans in terms of their own institution of *patroni* and *clientes*. This was a relationship based upon social duty: in return for the protection and personal support of a wealthy *patronus*, Roman *clientes* bound themselves solemnly to further his interests and perform his requests. The expression was accordingly used by Roman writers to convey Celtic clan relationship. But clan relationship also had an economic foundation, expressed in tenancy and rent. The chieftain and his principal followers lived upon their tenants' rents, whether in produce or stock; and the payment of such rents on large villa-estates, both in money and in kind, is shown upon the Moselle valley reliefs, already quoted as in other respects applicable to this side of the Channel. If the difference between the Romanized villas and the farms of primitive native style can be recognized as corresponding to the social distinction obtaining within the tribe between landowners and tenants, then its continuation may be explained by the freedom from interference which tribal custom enjoyed under Roman rule so long as the terms laid down by the treaty of settlement were observed.

This kind of relationship is the easier to recognize and accept, now that an old-established interpretation of native farm-sites has passed into oblivion. The thick clusters of huts and storage pits which go to make up the native farm used regularly to be interpreted as a village, since it was not then taken into account that these flimsy or unstable structures had short lives and were frequently renewed or discarded. In such settlements a complete and undifferentiated plan of all the remains gives an altogether misleading picture of activity, since in fact only a few of the features were in use at any given moment. The 'village', which was so common a feature on maps of Roman Britain, turns out to be a farm of the primitive type already well established in the island long before Roman rule, and an essential part of tribal economy. The broad distinction is to be drawn no longer between villas and villages, but between landowners of substance and their tenants or their neighbour smallholders. Further, while it is possible to deduce from archaeology the broad distinction only, Celtic story and legend indicate that the relationship must have been one of great variety, closely related to custom and individual grants or services on the one hand and strictly defined by tribal law upon the other. It has been shown by Mr C. E. Stevens how an extremely primitive type of tribal law concerning land-inheritance became in the fourth century A.D. the subject of a classic case in the highest Roman court of appeal.

The equipment of this kind of farm in corn-growing country is worth specification. The farm-house and accessory buildings form a group of huts either round or rectangular in plan. They are never large: an average cross-dimension of twenty feet would err on the high side. It has often been stated in the past that some were furnished with rude hypocausts, as if the inhabitants had borrowed central heating from the Roman world. But the alleged hypocausts do not occur in huts and are in fact corn-drying ovens; for the British farmer, as Pytheas had noted in the fourth century B.C., often gathered his corn green and threshed it under cover. This demands parching of the grain to make it keep. The plan of these kilns and their flues varied considerably, now bowl-shaped, now T-shaped, now H-shaped, and now forked. But the principle of construction was always the same, to create a fire whose hot gases passed through flues and heated gently a floor never itself in direct contact with the flame. Comparable installations, of much greater size and more complicated construction, are found in the Romanized villas. Once dried, the grain was stored in basket-lined pits. Both the pits and the corn-drying ovens needed frequent renewal, and a site occupied over a long period therefore yields them in bewildering multiplicity. The area of the farm is usually enclosed by a ditch and bank, and its comparative spaciousness, demanded in part at least by the room required for the various installations and their renewal, is again deceptive as an indication of either the peopling of the establishment or its capacity in output.

If the general social relationship of villas to small-holdings is clear, there are, however, many points upon which information is wholly lacking. It is known that in the southern area of Roman Britain the great plough, with massive coulter, was widely distributed, from Essex to Hampshire and Gloucestershire. These implements, first introduced in the Belgic area of pre-Roman Britain, are of uncertain form, but it is clear that while primitive methods of traction would enable them to be used in the smallest size of Celtic fields, 100 feet square, convenience would choose the larger sizes of field, up to 400 feet. The villas which were associated with this newer kind of agriculture may therefore be expected to have had a field-system of somewhat larger scale. This, however, has not yet been identified in detail, although the air-photographs of certain Oxfordshire villas, like

Ditchley and Little Milton, show clear traces of a new
lay-out of field boundaries to a generous scale in the
immediate vicinity of the farmhouse. On the other hand,
it may be regarded as equally certain that not a few conservative villa owners will have derived their wealth from
customary tenants engaged in farming in the old style,
and will therefore be in close touch, as are certain villas
north of Winchester, with unchanged field-systems of the
old type. How much there was of a new style in agriculture, and in what relationship it stood to the old, are thus
questions which can be asked but which must for the
time being remain unanswered. Still less has there been
detected any trace of the Roman fashion of centuriated
fields, systematically laid out in large standard rectangles
enclosed by a grid of accommodation roads. Such
systems might be expected to occur in the vicinity of the
coloniae at Lindum (Lincoln) or Glevum (Gloucester),
and Haverfield went so far as to indicate a parallel but
non-rectangular system of roads west of Camulodunum
(Colchester). But no unimpeachable example of centuriation has yet rewarded either the field-student or the
air-photographer. It seems evident that in the British
province Roman fields of the regular agrimensorial pattern were, to say the least, extremely rare, though their
identification has proved a will o' the wisp to many
antiquaries.

The rarity of application of the Roman system of field-
planning is emphasized by the practice observable over
many hundred thousands of acres in the Fenland. This
vast alluvial basin, famous for the fertility of its crops, has
in historic times always been so waterlogged as to require
extensive and systematic drainage for its development. In
more modern times the necessary combination of central
authority and skill was not found until the seventeenth

and later centuries; but the possibilities of the area did not escape the Romans, whose interest in the exploitation of marshland was sharpened by the value of such terrain in the Mediterranean soil and climate. The Fens were drained by a series of wide canals, the most notable being the Cambridgeshire and Lincolnshire Car Dykes, the latter over seventy miles long. In conjunction with the rivers, which in many places followed different lines from those of today, these canals served both for drainage and for transport. As drains, they acted as catch-waters, trapping the flow from the adjacent uplands and keeping it out of the Fens; and they were also linked with a complicated series of minor cuts which drained the Fens themselves. As canals, they linked the Fenland with the Witham at Lincoln, the Witham in turn being linked by means of the Fossdyke with the Trent. Access was thus obtained to the Humber and the Ouse, so that, as Stukeley long ago remarked, it was possible to proceed by inland waterways from the Fens to York. Stukeley further perceived that the importance of this connexion lay in the opportunity which it offered for the transport of the Fenland produce to military supply-depots.

The foundation of the system has been shown by excavation to belong to the later years of Nero; a date which has an important bearing upon the original design of the scheme and upon the origin of the labour force required both for the canals or drains and for the subsequent farming. At that time the Roman northern frontier was based upon Lincoln, and there was no reason for basic military supplies to proceed further. The construction of the Fossdyke canal to the Trent may well be an addition to the scheme, after the advance of the legionary base from Lindum (Lincoln) to Eburacum (York) in A.D. 71. As for the labour required to make them, the works are

RB—9

situated in land immediately adjacent to the territory of
the Iceni, and their construction belongs to the period
just after the revolt of A.D. 61, which the Iceni had led.
There can be little doubt that the conquered rebels were
condemned to labour at the new works and were thereafter drafted to the new agricultural reserve thus created,
working it upon terms much more favourable to Rome
than to themselves. It might, then, be thought that the
Romans would have imposed here their own system of
field-planning. But when the new fields and farms made
possible by the drainage are scrutinized upon the vast
mosaic of air-photographs by which the late Major Allen,
the Fenland Research Committee, and Dr St Joseph have
revealed them, it becomes clear that, while the canals and
the main roads across the area bear the systematic in-
print of the Roman engineer, the farms, fields, and lanes
are no less characteristically native. The conclusion is
inevitable that the natives, once planted upon the spot,
were left to work the land in their ancestral fashion, virtually no attempt being made to convert them to Roman
agricultural methods. Only the canal-side granaries indicate the stage at which the Roman tax-collector entered
into possession of the giant's share of the produce, and
that it was barged away to Roman depots.

The systematic excavation of a Fenland farm has yet
to be undertaken, just as certain forms of Fenland fields
or lazy-beds call for elucidation by the spade. But in
another area the brilliant reconsideration by Professor
Hawkes of the early but exquisitely precise excavations
undertaken by General Pitt-Rivers in Cranborne Chase
reveals both the farmsteads and the farmers' state of
servitude. When the number of storage-pits in use at one
time on such farms is compared with the number in use
under free enterprise in pre-Roman farms on similar soil,

it is calculated that under Roman rule the Cranborne Chase farmers were deprived of something like three-fifths of the yield, very different from the reasonable rates of taxation of one-twelfth or one-tenth which applied in other parts of the Roman world. It is not thought that the folk of this area were rebellious; but the Belgae, who owned it, had been violently hostile to Rome and hard fighting had been required to conquer them. In these circumstances the terms of capitulation will not have been merciful, and there are numerous analogies in the Roman world for punishment of an obstinate resistance by the reduction of the hostile populace to serfdom. But at least the native agriculturalist was left to pursue his own methods in field and farm unchanged.

That drastic changes could, however, be introduced is shown by the treatment accorded to the area in the later third century A.D. At this time many of the agricultural villages were deserted, and important instances appear of field-systems obliterated by a new class of large and systematically planned enclosures for cattle. The adjacent downland is also bordered by new dykes, which, when mapped in relation to timber-bearing soils, reveal themselves as delimiting ranch-land in relation to forests. This is a notable instance of a deliberate change in the planned economic development of government-controlled land. Cattle-raising and sheep-farming were substituted for ploughing; and it is to be observed that herds and flocks were among the famous features of British provincial economy by the opening of the fourth century A.D., when their qualities are extolled. With the sheep and their wool was connected cloth-production. This manufacture was also earning a reputation for Britain in the Roman world at large. The establishment of a government weaving-mill at Venta, mentioned in the *Notitia Dignitatum* or list of government appointments, may well be connected, if remotely, with these changes; for the Venta in question, whose tribe is not specified, is certainly to be identified with Venta Belgarum (Winchester). The cloth would be for the Services.

If in southern Britain there is some evidence of expansion of pastoralism at the expense of agriculture, in northern Britain the process was probably reversed. There is little evidence for agriculture on any scale but the smallest in the north in pre-Roman days. Indeed, it is noteworthy how the decorators of prized artistic objects choose either horses or cattle as their theme, both in pre-Roman and Roman days, and how cauldrons, for seething meat, continue to be one of the principal manufactures of the area. These facts imply a Homeric type of society or, if this be thought too sophisticated, a state of civilization akin to that of the Irish Celtic sagas, in which wealth is reckoned not in broad acres but in heads of cattle. Many of the upland native farms of Cumberland and Westmorland plainly continued to reflect these conditions. If they have any field-system, it comprises a limited number of tiny paddocks or crofts, unequal to supporting a family through the year. Their wealth and support lay in the adjacent hill-pastures, with valley feeding for the winter. But most of the cattle, as in medieval times, must have been killed off when the winter came, the most valuable arisings then being their hides and horns, convertible to leather and a variety of horn objects. The Roman tax-collector had a first interest in the herds, which were counted and taxed by heads: but his second and no less important interest lay in the hides. The consumption of hides by the Roman army must have been enormous. The jerkins and breeches of the soldiery, their shield-coverings and their tents, not to mention their massive boots, were all made of leather, and a tribute of hides will have been an obvious alternative to a tribute of corn. Excavation has suggested that leather was officially collected and tanned or tawed at Catterick. Thirdly, there was an interest in the carcass: for lard was part of the staple diet provided by the Roman government for its troops: and this too could be exacted from pastoral communities, whether cattle or pigs provided it.

One of the effects of the *pax Romana*, which stopped cattle-raiding between the different local groups, was to encourage an increase of population among the upland herdsmen of Westmorland and doubtless elsewhere. There came a time when the main settlements swarmed and minor farms grew up not far away, so that all the available land in the neighbourhood must have been pastured to the full. This is particularly evident in such a valley as that of the Lyvennet, south of Penrith, and other areas tell the same story. The increase did not necessarily spell prosperity for the individual: it may in fact have meant the reverse. But it did mean a rise in the amount of taxable property, when it came to counting animals, not to mention the possibilities of army recruitment.

There were, however, areas amid the fells and forests which show undeniable traces of a spreading agriculture. An outstanding example is Upper Wharfedale, where many miles of native field-systems exist, studded with native farms yielding Roman pottery and coins down to the close of the fourth century A.D. The Aire Gap was even opened to the villa system, though it must be significant that the single known example, at Gargrave in Craven, lies on the margin of an old glacial lake-bed, whose especially fertile land must have caught the eye of a wealthy man bent upon profitable farm-development. Similarly, the sole villa yet known in County Durham, at

Old Durham, lies upon the magnesian limestone belt, which still carries the best farming land in the area. Whether these establishments belonged to native land-owners or to Roman ex-soldier settlers must remain uncertain. But veteran settlers are known elsewhere in the north and it would be wrong to suppose that all the land-development was due to native enterprise. The fort of Bremetennacum Veteranorum (Ribchester, Lancashire) was the administrative centre of an enclave of veterans important enough to figure in a Roman geographical list. The Calder basin, from above Huddersfield to Castle-ford, has yielded altars dedicated to the tutelary deity of the Brigantes by Roman citizens whose names strongly suggest that they too were veteran settlers. Nothing, how-ever, is known of what form their settlements took or what kind of production was connected with them. If they were veterans then a land-settlement is most likely; and it should be observed that the Middle Gritstone, which the river Calder here cuts, supports good and comparatively light agricultural land.

Wharfedale and its upper basin are intimately related to an exceptional form of habitation, namely, the lime-stone cave-dwellings which are a feature of the Pennines and Peak District wherever geological conditions permit their existence. These dwellings have in the past been variously interpreted, but nearly always through the eyes of a civilized mentality which could conceive of them only as a refuge and not as a permanent dwelling. This, however, is not the view taken of such accommodation by peasant communities, to whom they offer a residence drier and more permanent than a hut, much warmer in winter and cooler in summer. It is therefore not surpris-ing that many of the caves, villages, and field-systems are intimately connected and that there is no real distinction to be drawn between the one and the other. They certainly do not represent the habitations of refugees from Roman rule, for most of them show a long continuity of habitation and they are not difficult either to find or to smoke out, as was the practice in Roman Africa when they were used by outlaws in this way. They represent rather the ready adaptation by man of advantages provided by Nature: an extra possibility in housing as opposed to an emergency measure.

Lake-dwellings are another specialized form of settlement which owe their existence to human adaptation of a natural feature. These are little known in Britain south of Hadrian's Wall, though they had existed during the pre-Roman Iron Age in the Somersetshire marshes, as the famous examples at Glastonbury and Meare attest. But in certain parts of southern Scotland, notably Galloway and Upper Clydesdale, they are well known in both the first and second centuries A.D. Unfortunately, most of the excavations of these very interesting but complicated northern structures were conducted when archaeological technique was less equal to dealing with them than it is today, and a modern examination of an untouched site is highly desirable. They normally comprise artificial islands or platforms built on the edge of lakes and carrying substantial timber huts. Their interest lies not merely in their structural details, but in the fact that their damp occupation layers frequently conserve intact perishable objects of wood, horn, and leather which the ordinary habitation site does not retain.

The varied scene of agricultural and pastoral activity provided by the numerous villas and farms demands for its completion the existence of markets and fairs: regional markets, held at comparatively frequent intervals, for the agricultural produce; fairs much less frequent and related to wider areas for the seasonal sales of animals. Within the canton, there might be several market-centres, and the cantonal capital need not necessarily have attracted the most important. The fairs might be so important as to attract folk from several cantons. But whenever or wherever they were held it is likely that in Britain, as throughout the ancient world, many were specifically associated with ancient sanctuaries whose deity hallowed the transaction and gave to the market or fairground a sacred peace which folk no less superstitious than quarrelsome would not violate by quarrels and brawls. The actual shrines where such gatherings may be detected are, however, few and detailed knowledge of them is still rare. Two may be cited, in widely separated districts.

The first is at Gosbecks Farm, three and a half miles south of Colchester, revealed by air-photography and since tested by excavation on a small scale. In its Roman guise, the place consisted of a temple of native pattern, the tall box-like shrine, with windows high above a veranda surrounding it, described in further detail below (p. 192). This building lay much off centre in a very large rectangle, bordered by a colonnaded enclosure, comprising two separate internal and external porticos, the internal designed to shelter worshippers, the external at the disposal of the general public. The planning indicates that, while the temple was undoubtedly important, other holy things, such as statues or venerated trees, occupied the sacred area; and that the area in question was an ancient pre-Roman holy place is demonstrated by the fact that the building had been substituted for an original large ditch, surrounding the same rectangular plot and containing pre-Roman rubbish. Outside the enclosure lay a great theatre, as at not a few sanctuaries in Roman Gaul, showing that crowds were expected and that their entertainment was catered for by stage performances secular or religious – a distinction very much more blurred in ancient times than now. As for deities, the place has yielded a beautiful bronze statue of Mercury, the god of trade and commerce, with classic stance but North-Gaulish features. The devotion to Mercury leaves no reasonable doubt of the association of this sanctuary with trade. The presence of large crowds suggests religious festivals combined with fairs or markets; while the native character and ancestry of the sanctuary dissociates it from the newly-introduced institutions of the adjacent Roman *colonia* and attaches it to local habit and tradition. It may be regarded as certain that Gosbecks was the scene of well-frequented fairs or markets, and the fact that it lay not far from the pre-Roman capital of the Trinovantes may be thought to have enhanced its importance.

The Gosbecks sanctuary was near a town. The second site lies in the open country at Woodeaton, north-east of Oxford, not far west of the half-way point along the Roman road between Dorchester on Thames and Alchester. These were both minor cantonal centres, on the borders of the Dobunni and Catuvellauni, and probably assignable to the latter. The place has long been renowned for the very large number of coins of small denomination found there, ranging from the early days of the province until the close of the fourth century A.D. Indeed, there were a few still later Roman coins, such as circulated during the fifth and sixth centuries A.D., as if the spot had continued to be frequented, as a remote centre in the backwoods very well might. A scatter of small votive objects, including miniature bronze axes, small bronze birds, and crudely modelled plaques, was associated with a well-built temple of native type in an irregular straight-sided enclosure occupying the low ridge which carries the site and lying somewhat below its summit. As at Gosbecks, it might seem that the temple stood to one side of the most significant point on the site, in this case the summit; but there is no clue as to what, if anything, stood there and it must be added that the highest point on the site was not included within the temple precinct. Nor is the deity or deities worshipped at Woodeaton known: among the votive objects a sort of duality can be detected, the axes suggesting a god with some characteristics at least of Mars, the birds a goddess. Celtic deities often went in pairs, and the cult objects, so far as they go, would suggest a pair like Sucellus and Nantosvelta, as opposed to Mercury and Rosmerta. Whoever they were, these deities attracted large crowds: and there is in addition a wealth of small objects that lie outside the range of offerings and suggest, no less strongly than the abundant small change, the existence of periodic fairs which thronged Woodeaton with buyers and sellers as well as worshippers.

In the north no such sites connected at once with commerce and religion are known to archaeology. But literature mentions the *Locus Maponi*, or meeting-place of Maponus, the Celtic god who was equated with the classical Apollo in his double aspect of youth and harper. This place may reasonably be identified with Clochmabenstane on the north shore of the Solway, where in later days the medieval English and Scottish wardens of the Marches met to settle common affairs. But the name is composite, half Brythonic and half English, *stane* having been added by Anglians who did not understand the Brythonic *cloch*. So the stone of Maponus was a traditional meeting-place, and in Roman frontier politics played its part as one of those permitted places of assembly for markets and public business which enabled Rome to control tribal gatherings. It is significant, too, that the god under whose auspices the assemblage took place was not a war-god, but a bardic god whose function was the peaceful entertainment of music. Other *loca* there were, but their names, where intelligible, are connected with tribes and not with deities, unless indeed the tribes, like the Brigantes, with their deity Brigans or Brigantia, had a guardian god or goddess whose name was identical with the adjectival form of their own.

Not all sanctuaries were connected with fairs and markets and the number of shrines scattered through the countryside must have been very large indeed. To describe them individually is quite outside the scope of this volume, though some of the cults associated with them are considered by themselves in another chapter. Here, however, certain classes may be mentioned since they must have formed one of the most characteristic features in the rural landscape, quite apart from the cult of which they formed the centre.

The most important is the pilgrim-sanctuary, of which the shrine of Nodens at Lydney, on the north side of the Severn estuary, provides a striking example. Nodens, who was sometimes equated by his worshippers with Silvanus, was certainly a god of hunting. But the bronze applied decoration on one of the ritual crowns of his ministrants shows that he was also a water-god, who journeyed majestically over the waves in a car drawn by four sea-horses: one thinks of the Severn bore, which begins near Lydney its formidable sweep at every tide. His temple, which belongs to after A.D. 364, occupies a prominent spur overlooking the estuary. It was a large building divided into nave and ambulatory, the latter equipped in due course with side-chapels. It was lavishly furnished

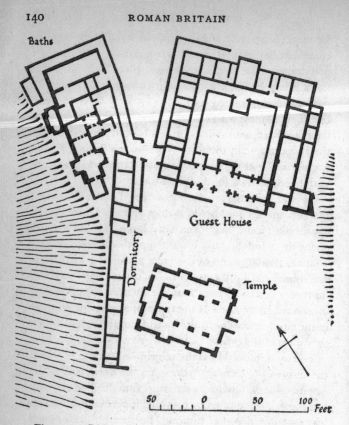

Figure 11. Lydney, the late-fourth-century pilgrim shrine
of Nodens

with mosaic pavements, the most important of which, in
the sanctuary, carried an inscribed dedication by the
chief of a naval repair-yard (*praefectus reliquationis*) and
a staff-interpreter. The plan of the building belongs to
neither the Celtic nor the purely classical world, but is a
form borrowed from the East; and the suggestion has
been made, without definite proof, that it owes some-

thing to Christian inspiration. The most interesting buildings, however, so far as the social side of the Lydney establishment is concerned, are those which surround the temple court, which occupies the whole of the hill-top. There is a long portico, rather like one side of a cloister, divided into open-fronted cells. This is a type of structure well-known in classical sanctuaries of healing, where the sick slept in hope of divine counsel through dreams or even of personal curative action by the god or his priests. On an adjacent site to that occupied by the portico lay a courtyard building with numerous rooms and a large and imposing front reception-hall. A commodious set of baths associated with this inn or guest-house add the essential hall-mark of Roman civilization. It is obvious that the establishment was planned for well-to-do visitors, who could pay good fees for attentions or benefits received. But not all the functions of Nodens were related to healing. As a god of hunting, he was expected by some of his worshippers to seek out and restore lost property, so that he was a god whose functions were hardly less diverse than his nature. Historically, the most interesting side of this cult is its late date, in an Empire slowly becoming Christian; and no less remarkable than this survival of paganism is the fact that in the last quarter of the fourth century A.D. a site of this kind, overlooking the Bristol Channel, could be considered a safe and even lucrative proposition. The status of one of its important patrons as a naval officer is a pointed reminder of the fleet to which the district owed its peace and safety.

The temple of Nodens lies on a hill-top and within the lines of an ancient hill-fort. It was thus with another late-Roman sanctuary, which was established, again after A.D. 364, in the long-deserted but gloriously imposing hill-fort of Maiden Castle, the ancient Dunum, which

had been superseded by the Romanized town of Durnonovaria in the seventies of the first century A.D. The
shrine built here was a simple edifice of the box-like
Celtic plan, though the deity worshipped therein combined with a human nature the wisdom and the strength
respectively of an owl and a bull. Side by side with the
shrine lay a small priest's house. The furnishings of the
temple had been costly, and included imported marble,
but there is no hint here of accommodation for pilgrims
or the like, although the place was in fact much less
remote than Lydney from a civilized community. It may
well be asked what general notion prompted the late
establishment of sanctuaries in the old deserted high
places? There are other examples, as at Lydney, Chanc-
tonbury Ring (Sussex), and Harlow Hill (Essex), and it
can hardly be doubted that more existed. Was it the final
flicker of paganism, or a turning to the old gods in centres
of ancient valiance as times grew more uncertain? Or
were the ancient gods taking refuge in the wilderness as
Christianity spread in the towns? In some places, indeed,
the old gods remained firmly in possession of their pre-
Roman shrines. This state of affairs, already noted at
Gosbecks, is exemplified by Frilford, north-west of Abing-
don, where two Romanized shrines lie on top of an
earlier wooden building. The pre-existing building had
taken the form of a circular ditched enclosure containing
an open covered shed, like a *presepio*, where holy images,
cult objects, or offerings had been exposed to view. In the
Roman period this earlier shrine was razed to the ground
and replaced by a circular enclosure of which the contents are not now evident, while a new temple of the
native box-like form was built alongside and later
received an extension. Occupation of this site continued
into the fifth century A.D. and there can be no doubt

either of the antiquity or the popularity of this country shrine or group of shrines. As a group, of which other members perhaps remain to be discovered, it resembles the forest sanctuaries of Roman Gaul, where numerous godlings attracted long and late to a single holy spot their several groups or categories of worshippers.

Wayside shrines form another common class. Such are the Surrey temples at Titsey on the Downs, adjacent to the Roman road between London and the Ouse valley, and again at Farley Heath, Aldbury. Of different type are shrines and pavilions, which yielded a relief of Diana and a hound and an altar to Apollo Cunomaglus, situated on the Fosse Way at Nettleton Shrub, ten miles north-east of Bath. The Watling Street shrines at Barkway (Hertfordshire), sacred to Mars Alator, and at Stony Stratford (Buckinghamshire), dedicated to Toutates, produced the beautiful silver plaques now in the British Museum, but no building which has been recorded. North of Lancaster, the shrine of Ialonus, god of the meadow-land, which again is known from an altar and not from buildings, lay close to the Roman road heading for the fort at Watercrook, near Kendal.

Spring and river-gods also had their sacred dwellings. At Chester-le-Street, Condatis, god of the watersmeet, had an altar at the confluence of the River Wear and the Cong Burn. Verbeia, goddess of the River Wharfe, was worshipped at Ilkley. No temple at the source of a great river is known in Britain, but it can hardly be doubted that they existed, particularly when rivers frequently bore divine names, such as Belisama (the Ribble), Deva (the Dee), or Brigantia (the Brent).

A hunter's shrine at Nettleton Shrub has already been mentioned. More romantic relics of ancient hunting are the shrines of Silvanus which sprang up in lonely cloughs on the high moors of the Pennines. These were erected by the commandants of Roman forts, wealthy men, mostly on the first rungs of their careers in the Imperial Civil Service, to commemorate successful hunting expeditions. Two are attested by altars only: one stone dedicated by Aurelius Quirinus, commandant at Lanchester (Co. Durham) and found at Eastgate in Weardale; the other erected by Sabinianus, commandant of a cavalry regiment, in remote Bollihope, 'after catching a lovely boar which previous hunters had hunted in vain'. The third, boasting both altars and shrines, lay higher still, on the Eller Beck, south of Bowes (Yorkshire), 1,275 feet above sea-level. There the local commandant, Caesius Frontinus, and one of his centurions set up separate shrines to Vinotonus, a stream-god whom the centurion identified with Silvanus. The temples were simple structures, one round and the other rectangular, with stone walls and thatched roofs. Their ruins still half buried the altars when they were first observed by a shepherd. If this could obtain after seventeen centuries, how manifestly grim and true must have been the allusion of Gildas in the sixth century A.D. to the ruins of shrines everywhere, 'their walls, inside and out, bristling with weathered idols of savage mien'. His phrase reveals in startling fashion the effect of belief in a multiplicity of deities upon the landscape of the countryside when the power of heathendom was exalted.

Sacred groves are archaeologically unresponsive, though the planning of many temple enclosures seems to imply their existence. But place-names in Britain indicate a very few of the many there must have been. The Celtic word for such a spot was *nemeton*, which is explained in an ancient glossary as meaning, in the plural, *sacra silvarum*, 'the holy places of the woods'. It occurs in Cornwall or

south-west Devon in the name Nemetotatio, in Monmouthshire in the form (Ne)metambala, and in Derbyshire as Aquae Arnemetiae, the name for Buxton, in
which the second element applies to the goddess dwelling
'over against the *nemeton*'. The Buxton grove no doubt
overshadowed the source of the healing waters. A little
farther south, on the Fosse Way in Nottinghamshire,
Vernemeton, means 'the great grove' according to the
Gaulish bishop Venantius Fortunatus. Finally, in Scotland, not far from the Antonine Wall, there is Medione-
meton 'middle-grove' or 'mid-way grove', which has been
identified, attractively but not with complete certainty,
with a prehistoric sanctuary at Cairnpapple (West
Lothian).

Lastly, there are the tombs and cemeteries. Folk in
Britain had for long ages been used to great tombs as
features of the landscape. The habit of according prominent positions to barrows of the Bronze and Iron Ages
ensured that few sky-lines were without these arresting
land-marks. The outsize in all barrows, Silbury Hill,
formed the sighting point for the Roman road from
Mildenhall (Wiltshire) to Bath. It should, however, be
remembered that the habit of building these circular
tumuli continued into Roman times, and that Roman
roads in certain parts of Britain, as in the Meuse basin in
north-eastern Gaul, were frequently lined with them.
The Six Hills at Stevenage are a famous group, by the
side of the western loop of Ermine Street. The road from
Salisbury to Dorchester is flanked by three at Badbury
Rings. But these last are outliers. The great concentration is in East Anglia, where these barrows certainly
carry on the traditions of an Iron-Age aristocracy, whose
rich tumuli, opulently furnished with imports from the
Roman world, are so notable a feature of the area in the

first half of the first century A.D. For these people, however, it was the content of the tomb and luxurious objects
buried with the dead which were important; for example,
the official chairs buried at Holborough (Kent) and
Bartlow (Essex). From the Roman point of view the
external aspect of the monument was also highly significant; not for sombre grandiosity, as in monuments of the
Republic, nor for religious symbolic ornament, as in
tombs of the later Empire, but for relief sculpture giving
a lasting picture of the daily life and avocations of the
deceased, as it were a record of their very being. In Gaul
such monuments, which took their form from the Mediterranean world, occasionally survive, as at Igel, in the
Moselle valley. On this famous example the daily life,
and, less prominently, the work, of a rich family engaged
in cloth-production covers the panels and friezes of a
lofty and slender monument crowned by a very high and
concave roof, almost like a crocket; and mixed with these
secular representations are the myths of Hercules, ex-
pressing the religious beliefs of the family as well. Britain
retains no such monument. But it must be recalled that
knowledge of the majority of those in Gaul is derived
from the use of their sculptured blocks and slabs in
the foundations of late-Roman walls. The only walls in
Britain which have as yet yielded materials of this kind
in abundance are the London bastions and the Constan-
tian north wall of Chester. The former happen to have
yielded early monuments only, the great altar tomb of
the procurator Classicianus, and soldier's monuments
from near the fort of the standing garrison. The latter
produced a variety of material from a most interesting
series of small monuments but nothing on the grand scale,
for vast and costly tombs could hardly be expected outside a legionary fortress. It would, however, be rash to

suppose that monuments of the Igel scale never existed in southern Britain. The foundations of an elaborate circular tomb set in the middle of a small cemetery at Harpenden (Hertfordshire) reveal a central, niched tomb-chamber containing at least one life-sized statue; while its angle-pilasters imply a decorative treatment of the front with the round tower-like structure rising above. Another very large tomb was the circular mausoleum at West Mersea (Essex), a stone-revetted structure with earth fill, sixty-five feet in diameter, braced by radiating walls and marginal buttresses. A circular mausoleum, thirty feet in diameter, with external buttresses, occurs at Keston (Kent) in association with a villa. A square tower-tomb, standing in a large precinct, is known at Corbridge (Northumberland). Other country districts have yielded walled cemeteries. That at Harpenden (Hertfordshire), already noted, was walled. But Kent boasts of at least six, among which Lockham contained two monumental tombs, Plaxtol a barrow, Sittingbourne a monumental tomb, and Springhead, near Southfleet, some very rich finds, including elaborate shoes of purple leather ornamented with gold thread. The reason why such monuments do not survive in the south-eastern districts of the island, devoid of good building-stone, is that folk of later ages seized upon the Roman stonework with avidity.

Roman triumphal monuments in the open country-side would be rare. But the foundations of a famous one exist at Rutupiae (Richborough), the principal port of entry to the province. They form an enormous base 30 feet deep below ground level, 145 feet long and 105 feet wide, including a flange for a few steps. The structure which was thus carried was cased in Carrara marble and its main columns were not less than 50 feet high. There may well have been a second stage above this and there were certainly some massive bronze statues, of which small fragments have been found. The monument was built about A.D. 80–100 and evidently commemorated peace established in the province. It is comparable with the Tetrapylon or four-way arch erected in honour of Claudius at two points of entry to the province of Egypt, and this may well have been the actual form of the monument. Later, towards the close of the third century A.D., it was stripped of its ornaments and served as a fortified look-out post against Saxon pirates, a choice no doubt determined by its great height.

No other monument of the kind can be tied to a specific site. But inscribed blocks from a monument commemorating the erection of Hadrian's Wall were used in building the Saxon monastery church at Jarrow (Co. Durham). An Italian marble head of provincial style found at Hawkshaw, in the wilds of the Upper Tweed basin, is more problematic. It cannot have come from far away, its Roman date is not in doubt and its occurrence is perhaps least difficult to explain by connecting it with a triumphal monument; of which, however, structural remains have not been identified.

CHAPTER FOUR

ECONOMICS

WHEN the geographer Strabo, writing early in the principate of Tiberius (A.D. 14–38), but recording many things of a generation or two earlier, gives an account of British exports to the Continent, he reflects conditions in south-eastern Britain and particularly the exports at the disposal of tribal chiefs and their followers. Corn, cattle, hides, and hunting-dogs attest the agriculture and stock-raising of Sussex, Kent, and Essex. Slaves represent the profit of raiding expeditions on the fringe of these areas. The metals, however, must have come from further afield: silver from the Mendip or Peak lead deposits; tin from Cornwall, gold from Wales, and iron from the Forest of Dean or the Weald. The trade in metals implies, in fact, as in prehistoric days, particular connexions more widely developed. The statement reverses, too, the hasty conclusion of Cicero, derived from his brother on Caesar's staff, that there was in Britain 'not so much as a scruple of silver'.

Metals in any province were almost exclusively State property, and formed an important item in the provincial budget. In Britain, the principal metal product was lead, which sounds dull, until it is recalled that the only way of producing silver known to the ancient world was by cupellation from lead, and that the abundant British lead represents a by-product from silver extraction. In the Roman world silver was the most regular money of account, and the need for large quantities explains the rapid development of British lead resources, attested by the numerous date-stamped ingots, or pigs, of the metal. The Mendip mines were in production by A.D. 49, six years after the conquest, the Flintshire mines by A.D. 74, the mines of Nidderdale, Yorkshire, by A.D. 81. All these dated pigs, and most others, are from direct Imperial working, but some undated examples from Derbyshire, and one early but undated example from Flintshire, bear the stamps of lessees, all Roman mercantile citizens. Rarer still, but again associated with the Derbyshire area, are the pigs of the Lutudarum Partners (*socii Lutuda-renses*) which took the name from the principal centre in the mining district, perhaps Chesterfield, and dispatched pigs in large numbers by water to the Humber. The quantity of lead extracted from Britain was very great and the Romans were struck by the ease with which it could be mined. The elder Pliny refers to much open cast mining. But he adds a significant and curious fact, that production was restricted in favour of the Spanish market. This is one of the rare cases in which such artificial controls are known to have been applied, though similar action was taken to restrict vine-growing in Gaul.

Of working and organization very little is known. In the Mendips the principal centre was Charterhouse on Mendip, where the remains of a mining settlement cover a considerable area and are graced by a small amphitheatre. An early pig from this area is countermarked by the Second Legion and this might suggest soldiers in charge of convict labour, for relegation to the mines was in the Roman world a form of penal servitude. But no evidence exists either way in the Mendips for the continuity of this practice, if it was in fact there applied. The Imperial stamped ingots continue until A.D. 164–9, though some are countersigned with private companies' marks, while another carries the name of C. Nipius

Ascanius, a Roman freedman lessee, also known in Flintshire. After that they appear no more, and it may well be that the working of the mines was then delegated to the *curiales* or tribal council, or to private concessionaires. This at least became the practice in other important Roman mining areas. If so, it would certainly account for the abundance of late-Roman silver coinage in the Somersetshire area, since the *curiales* would be receiving a substantial percentage of the output, returned to them in the form of silver coinage. In the fourth century A.D. Britain was still famous for its metal output, and the quantity of pewter and lead objects belonging to the period bears witness to its copiousness.

In the earlier period of Imperial working there is some evidence for the export of Mendip lead. The pig countermarked by the Second Legion was found at St Valéry-sur-Somme, while one occurs at Stockbridge (Hampshire) and two on the Solent. This suggests a traffic of consignments across the Channel and along the main arterial route to Southern Gaul or Italy. It is not likely, however, as the administrative fragmentation of the Empire developed, that this traffic continued brisk.

The earliest stamped pig associated with Flintshire is of A.D. 74; and, if the annexation of the area occurred in A.D. 61, there would be evidence for rapid exploitation, as in the Mendips. The Italian concessionaire, C. Nipius Ascanius, cannot be much later, since his countermark appears on a Mendip pig of A.D. 59. The centre of the actual mining seems to have been Halkyn Mountain, as today, while the mining settlement lay at Pentre Ffwrndan, one mile south-east of Flint, where pottery and coins suggest an occupation beginning about A.D. 70 and continuing until at least the close of the second century A.D. There is also some evidence, though it is not strong, for third-century exploitation at Meliden, at the northern tip of the Clwydian mountains, in the Talar Goch mine. It would be interesting to know whether this was the reason for the foundation of the adjacent military site at Prestatyn, on a then navigable coastal creek. The pigs from the Flintshire area are stamped *Deceangl,* for *metallum Deceanglicum,* the name surviving in the medieval district of Tegeingl and today in a deanery. This was the name of the tribe which the manuscript of Tacitus presents as Decangi, the metropolitan version of a name which must have seemed oddly barbaric to a Latin ear.

The next dated group of lead pigs is the small group from Yorkshire, which also carry the tribal name of the area, in the form *Brig,* for *metallum Briganticum.* They are found in the area between Nidderdale and Wharfedale, which was much exploited in later medieval times for lead also. The earliest dated example is of A.D. 81, exactly ten years after the Roman acquisition of the area. Another, of Trajan (A.D. 98–117), is imperfectly recorded from Pateley Bridge. It is probable that this was not the only lead-bearing area worked in Yorkshire. There is a good local tradition of Roman exploitation of the Swaledale lead deposits, in particular the Hurst Mine; it is connected with a pig of Hadrian, unfortunately never recorded in detail.

The Derbyshire lead field is one of the largest and most productive in Britain. There is evidence for Imperial working under Hadrian, but in addition many undated pigs are stamped with the names of private lessees. The fact that these names have a first-century ring about them does not definitely exclude a later date. The Roman name of the field or its centre, was Lutudarum and appears also as qualifying the name of a private com-

pany, the *socii Lutudarenses*. At what stage, however,
the *socii* occur or in what order they came in relation
either to the individual lessees or the Imperial working,
or whether, again, all or any two were contemporary, is
quite unknown. It may be observed, however, that the
socii sent down their pigs in large numbers to Petuaria
(Brough on Humber), either to their own warehouse or to
local wholesalers. Yet another aspect of exploitation is the
lead ore from stream deposits found in the Roman fort at
Navio (Brough on Noe), from which the district was in
part policed. This implies a system of collection by
natives for which the fort served as central depot. The
whole picture in Derbyshire is thus a complicated one.
The relationship of the various elements is obscure; the
administrative centre of the field is not fixed, though it is
named, and the duration of the exploitation is unknown.
This makes the record tantalizing and leaves only an
abiding impression of intensive activity in an area attractive to the Imperial agent and the commercial speculator
alike. Hadrianic working of lead is also attested in south-
west Shropshire, in the Shelve and Snailbeach areas.
Here or in Flintshire the Twentieth Legion took some
hand in organization of the mining, since it countermarked at least one pig, found at Châlon-sur Saône and
dated to A.D. 195. Beyond this, however, there is no evidence for later Imperial working, and it may be that the
field was turned over to concessionaires or small lessees.
It is, on the other hand, likely that the small but rich
field on the eastern slopes of Plynlimon, under development during the second century A.D., was always worked
by the military.

Military supervision was certainly exercised in the
Alston lead-mines of south-west Northumberland, which
were worked upon a smaller scale in the third century

A.D. under the Second Cohort of Nervii. Stamped seals from consignments which reached Brough under Stainmore bear the name of the cohort and the legend '*metal(lum)*'. It is likely that some of the produce also went north-eastwards to Corstopitum (Corbridge), where the mineral wax associated with the Alston veins has been found. The fort of Caermote (Cumberland) seems to have been a collecting centre for lead from the adjacent fells. Another lead-mining settlement associated with the military is Machen (Glamorganshire), where a settlement and remains of workings have been observed. It need hardly be doubted that in the military areas there were other ventures of the kind, since the Imperial government came to develop local resources wherever possible. The pawky request of Nero's legionaries that 'commanders looking for silver should get their decorations in advance' would indeed have been out of date.

If the exploitation of lead may be regarded as of great importance both in itself and in relation to silver extraction, the copper workings of Britain were also of substantial value in themselves and in their relation to bronze, an alloy used in the Roman world for almost every hard-wearing purpose. The principal deposits of copper lay in the north-west, in northern Shropshire, Caernarvonshire, and Anglesey. The Shropshire deposit is centred at Llanymynech, where the cave from which the veins have been worked by galleries was apparently inhabited by the miners.

Similar conditions appear to have existed in the Caernarvonshire copper mines of Great Orme's Head, where inhabited caves have also been noted, and associated objects date the activity to the third and fourth centuries A.D. This cave dwelling again suggests labourers tied to the spot, whether they were slaves or convicts, but it seems that no smelting was done on the spot, the ore being carried away for treatment elsewhere. The copper cakes found in Caernarvonshire are stamped with the names of at least two private companies; and this would support exploitation by slave labour, though it is not necessarily true for every mine or for every period. In Anglesey the picture is rather different. Here the principal mining area was Parys Mountain near Amlwch, though other activity is known, as at Aberffraw and Pengarnedd. But the copper cakes in the island are all associated with native villages, as if the ore were gathered by native labour and smelted piecemeal in the villages for eventual collection at a central depot. This would imply that the island, once the cult centre of the Druids, was treated as a temple estate with a fixed tribute transferred from the Druidical community to the Roman State. The mines will explain the continuing interest of the Romans in the fort at Caernarvon (Segontium) and the provision of a naval station in the harbour at Holyhead in order to protect the valuable raw material and its workers from pirates, or slave-raiders. It is significant that while there is no evidence for legionary occupation at Chester after A.D. 367, the Caernarvon fort was then re-occupied intensively, the occupation lasting until A.D. 383. Its cessation is connected in Welsh legend with not only the usurpation but the actual person of Magnus Maximus, in the guise of Maxen Wledig. Whatever the truth of the story, it at least coincides with the archaeological facts and with the economic value of the copper deposits. It should be emphasized that these are the most northerly and the most important copper deposits exploited by the Romans in Britain. The Cheshire mines at Alderley Edge do not appear to have been worked in Roman times, though well known to prehistoric and medieval man. The Yorkshire deposits at Middleton Tyas were too deep and too waterlogged and were only accessible after the advent of steam pumping-machinery.

Much the most famed of British metals in the days before the Roman occupation was tin. The vivid accounts by Diodorus Siculus, of overland pack-horse transport of Cornish tin from the Gallic coast to Narbo (Narbonne) in the first century B.C., and of the island emporium on the British coast, from which merchants obtained it, all speak of a brisk and flourishing early trade, monopolized in Caesar's day by the Veneti of Brittany. But in the Augustan age, when the conquest of north-western Spain made the Spanish tin deposits available, commercial interest in British tin ceased, while the anti-Roman refugee warriors from Gaul who were crowding into south-west Britain cannot have encouraged adventurers. Even when the island became a province and the Dumnonii one of the philo-Roman allied communities, it does not appear that the Roman government took much interest in developing the tin. There is slight evidence for activity in the first century A.D.: somewhat later the best evidence is the occurrence of two *stationes*, or Treasury Offices, in the area, presumably connected with the working or leasing of stannaries. The source which mentions them used for Britain material of the second century A.D. But only in the third century A.D., and particularly after the ruin of the Spanish mines in its last quarter, does Government interest in the area begin. Milestones from Gordian III (A.D. 244–9) onwards, with a special outburst of activity under Constantine and his house, attest new efforts in development. It is significant that now commences a very wide distribution of pewter table services; later in the century blocks of pewter with official stamps from the Thames at Battersea attest cargoes of

this valuable metal being concentrated in London, the
seat of the provincial Treasury administration. How late
the development continued is not known. But it is a
remarkable fact that in the sixth century A.D. a storm-
blown Byzantine ship could unload its corn and relieve a
famine in Exeter and return with a cargo of tin, as if the
merchant adventurers of the Dark Ages were repeating
the experiences of prehistoric man.

After tin came gold. Only one gold mine of the Roman
age is known in Britain, at Dolau Cothi, near Pumpsaint,
between Llanio and Llandovery in north-east Caermarthenshire, among the Demetae. Here the workings are
both open-cast and by long and deep adits, following the
veins of gold-bearing pyrites. The adit galleries are very
systematically cut, to serve for both drainage and haulage,
and in the levels below them wheels for lifting water
were installed to drain them, as in the Spanish mines. A
panning cradle has also been found. At the shaft-head
the ore was pounded, milled, and washed, a good head of
water for the latter purpose being brought in a special
aqueduct or open lade some eight miles long. A bath-
house is also known, reminiscent of that mentioned in *lex
metalli Vipascensis*, but in fact seems to belong to a fort. The
scale of working certainly attests either Government
activity or a concessionaire company of high standing and
efficiency. The date is not defined, though some gold
jewellery made on the spot is of late-second- or early-
third-century style. A detailed study of this most interesting scene of specialized Roman development is overdue.

The iron mines of Britain were numerous and hardly
less productive than the lead mines. Iron was not ac-
counted a valuable metal nor was its output restricted,
for it is clear that there was always a good market for so
useful a commodity. The principal deposits exploited by

Rome lay in the Weald and the Forest of Dean. The former was being rapidly developed under Claudius and Nero by the native client-king Cogidumnus at Chichester, with a guild of iron-workers organized in Roman fashion. It is tempting to think that this represents the Romanization of a group of native smiths, who must already have had a special position in prehistoric economy. How the deposits were exploited when the native kingdom passed out of existence is unknown, but coins and pottery from many sites cover the whole Roman period. Very large quantities of slag and cinders were available for local road construction; and this might suggest that the *curiales* continued to develop the deposits in succession to the native king, using its by-product for road-making which was also a communal concern. Direct interest of the provincial government in some at least of the iron-workings is, however, suggested by the occurrence of the official stamped roofing-tiles of the *Classis Britannica*, or Fleet in Britain, in connexion with slag near Wadhurst (Sussex). No administrative or working centre for the Weald is known. In the Forest of Dean, however, much working was concentrated at Weston-under-Penyard (Ariconium), where earlier antiquaries noted an area of 200 acres covered with slag-heaps. Here exploitation can hardly have developed until after the conquest of the Silures in A.D. 74–6: the coins indicate activity from the late first century A.D. until the fourth, with a marked increase towards the end.

The iron-stones of Northamptonshire and Lincolnshire, and the beds of iron nodules in Norfolk, were developed. There are large slag deposits and workshops, almost unexplored, at Clipsham; while a Roman blast-furnace has been noted at Woolsthorpe near Colsterworth and working deposits adjacent to Scunthorpe. In Norfolk a blast-furnace is known at Ashwicken. In Yorkshire, large heaps of clinker at West Bierley, near Cleckheaton, were associated with coins of the late third and early fourth centuries A.D. Further north still, the military workshops at Corbridge, active in the third and fourth centuries A.D., were using low-grade smeltings from native hearths. These blooms were then re-smelted in puddling furnaces for ultimate forging into weapons, nails, and hold-fasts produced in the workshops. The source of the material was the Redesdale deposits, just south of the fort of Habitancum (Risingham), used again much later for Armstrong's early munition works on Tyneside. This picture of a military arsenal is unique in the Roman world.

Coal was also mined in Roman Britain, though it never became, as far as is known, an item of export: and British coal is only mentioned once in Roman literature, as a curiosity seen upon the altars of Sulis Minerva at Aquae Sulis (Bath). Its tendency 'to become round stone masses' will be noted with a smile. This was undoubtedly the Somersetshire cannel coal. But the Nottinghamshire coal has been noted in the Fenland villages. Local coals, microscopically identical with local veins, have been noted on Hadrian's Wall in a Benwell fort smithy, at Housesteads and Corbridge: and their use is dated to the second century A.D. at the first and last places and to the fourth century A.D. at the last two. It was also used in the second century A.D. on the Antonine Wall, at Castlecary and Bar Hill forts; while less detailed observations attest coal in Roman forts at Risingham, South Shields, and Manchester. In industry coal was used for smelting lead at Pentre Ffwrndan, iron and glass at Wilderspool, and iron at Weston-under-Penyard, and for heating hypocausts at Wroxeter and Caerwent. It must, however, be recognized that wood or charcoal were the fuels much more normally employed and that coal was used only where it was handier to get than wood. In the Fenland, to quote an extreme case, it would arrive as ballast in the barges and be transported much more easily in the canal system than logs.

Three other natural deposits provided not fuel but ornaments. The Kimmeridge shale of the Isle of Purbeck, in Dorset, was worked extensively into jewellery, decorative panels, and furniture. The personal decorations consist principally of lathe-turned bracelets, from which the cores were so numerous as to win the name of 'Kimmeridge money'. But the material could also be cut and carved in sheets, forming panels after the fashion of marble veneering, or, when lightly hollowed, flat dishes or trays. These table furnishings were modelled upon metal prototypes, just as were Victorian trays of papier-mâché, though the hardness of the shale suited the treatment better. Even furniture was thus made, table-legs with claw-feet and sea-horse or sea-lion shoulders being known and widely distributed in southern Britain, though not common. Furniture of this kind must have been difficult and hazardous to manufacture, and consequently both expensive to buy and frail to maintain, though it could be kept in good condition by oiling. It should be observed, however, that whenever this material is decoratively carved, its patterns run upon very strictly classical lines, as if the firm operating the concession was Roman in its emphasis, not to hazard a guess at its origin. A detailed study of this very interesting Romano-British industry is still wanting.

The second natural deposit is Purbeck marble. This was much used for mortars in which a very hard grinding or pounding surface was required, and vessels of this des-

cription are found very widely distributed over the province though more thickly near the source. It was also
used to make tablets for important inscriptions, as far
afield as Noviomagus (Chichester), Corinium (Cirencester), Verulamium (St Albans), Camulodunum (Colchester), Londinium (London), and Deva (Chester). The
variety favoured was greyish-white in colour, and formed
a particularly handsome speckled background to the ver-
milion lettering in cinnabar (*minium*) favoured in Roman
monumental inscriptions. Panels and mouldings for
decoration are well known and widely distributed, both
in town and country, also lavers for public baths, as at
Calleva (Silchester).

The third natural deposit is jet, associated with the
Whitby lias, wherein it is found as lumps. Solinus describes British jet with interest, as a substance heated with
water but quenched with oil and magnetic when rubbed.
These paradoxical qualities endowed jet with almost
magical esteem, and it became a favourite material for
ornamental jewellery, much of which was manufactured
at Eburacum (York). Hair-pins, spindles, finger-rings,
and bracelets were made in great variety, some bracelets
and many necklaces being ingeniously articulated in
minute component pieces. Elaborately carved pendants
and medallions, including family groups executed to
order, and teddy-bears, represent other profitable lines of
production. Whether the jet articles of the Rhineland
represent imports from Britain or local working of the
British raw material is difficult to estimate: but it can at
least be said that there are few Rhenish products un-
matched in Britain, and that jet does not form an item of
Rhineland exportation to free Germany. As in the objects
of Kimmeridge shale, the artistic tone of these productions,
British or Rhenish, is essentially Roman, and native motifs

are wholly absent. This Roman jet-working differs in finish from the modern Victorian, by refraining from high polish: the effect is rather of soft burnishing, certainly more attractive to sensitive taste.

Other natural products for which Britain won a modest fame were jewels. British pearls were of some repute, though their duskiness was deprecated. They were found both in rivers and on the sea-shore and were apparently not gathered from living oysters. Scottish rivers, in particular the Aberdeenshire Dee, have in more recent times produced large examples. Amethysts were also won from an island in the Western ocean; and an island yielding gems is once mentioned in geography. The trade in hunting-dogs also continued, and three breeds at least are known in literature: the Irish wolf-hound, seven of which caused a stir in Rome when Symmachus exhibited them; the bull-dog, known to Claudian; and a small spaniel described in some detail by Oppian. The favourite dogs of the Castor ware potters, however, are of greyhound breed, like Diana's dog at Nettleton Shrub, and this would indicate a fourth variety. Bears were also exported, mostly for the arena, where they were already under Domitian used for lacerating criminals. In the fourth century A.D., when Claudian seeks a characteristic dress for a personification of north Britain, he gives her a bear-skin. If he had chosen a seal-skin the conception would have been equally apt, for the pelts of these creatures, in which Britain abounded, were both much prized and highly priced in the Roman world. Furs and skins must have formed an important export.

Such British cloth as was famous abroad was probably of a special kind: the *birrus Britannicus* of Diocletian's price-list was a rain-cloak, the *tapete* a rug or horse-cloth; and glossaries say that the cloth for *birri* was of goats' wool.

But on the home market of the province there was certainly much sheeps' wool available; the fourth-century panegyrist praises the flocks laden with fleeces, and there can be no doubt that numerous estates were engaged in wool production. The fine pair of cropping shears from Great Chesterford, now at Cambridge, can only have come from a woollen-mill, though their function, to give the piece a firm nap, has now for long been performed by machinery. At Silchester a small dye-works was excavated, though its date within the Roman period remains uncertain. Linen is nowhere specifically mentioned, but its use on a large scale for finely woven shrouds in the York district should be noted.

Food-stuffs are not recorded as regularly exported. But corn-export in A.D. 361 to the Rhineland is shown by the context as not an emergency measure. Oysters also, though not unknown to Italian epicures of the first century A.D., can hardly have travelled in quantity, and some senators at least must have tasted them in Britain itself. They formed, however, a very large trade within the province. Few Roman sites are without them and it is clear that in taverns and shops outside the fortresses and forts of the province the oyster-bar was the Romano-British equivalent of the modern fried-fish shop. Mussels are on many sites almost equally numerous, and were no doubt cheaper, if less luscious.

Among British home industries, the best known, even though much more awaits discovery, are the potteries. The most renowned are those at Durobrivae (Castor on Nene), excavated in desultory fashion in the nineteenth century by Artis and only now being seriously studied. These potteries turned out a great variety of vessels, though drinking-cups form the principal item. They are somewhat coarser in proportion than the Rhenish wares;

the clay of which they are made fires to a lighter colour, and their finish is less brilliant or glossy. Their decoration in barbotine, is, on the other hand, of perhaps greater variety: the favourite conventional pattern is a running scroll of ivy-leaves, no doubt borrowed from contemporary plainer forms of Samian ware, but normally executed with a sure and sweeping touch which the more rigid Samian lacks. Very common, and animated by the same fresh and rapid handiwork, are the so-called Hunt cups, in which swift dogs chase hares or deer. Human scenes include chariot-races, gladiatorial combats, and, occasionally, scenes from classical mythology, while sometimes the place of humans or animals is taken by phallic emblems of good luck. The human scenes are seldom successful by classical standards. The very nature of the barbotine technique, by which the figures were traced in wet clay like icing sugar, made it impossible to catch the subtleties of the human form and denied to the artist the control of outline obtainable by incised technique or by carefully prepared moulds. It would have been wiser to be less ambitious, yet the ambition is of a kind which occurs in no other province. It is British in character, as stubbornly determined as our imitations of Chinese wares in a later age; and perhaps the most interesting side of the attempt is that this development should have been thought necessary to attract a market. It reflects, socially speaking, a purchasing public gladdened by hunting, racing, and stories of divine adventures. But while there is a vivid appeal to the imagination, there is no appeal to literacy. No attempt was made to imitate the inscribed wares of Rhenish manufacture. Further, the figured wares, today attracting most attention, formed in fact only a small part of the output. There was a large series of drinking cups, wholly undecorated or at most provided with scales on shoulder and side, to prevent the vessel from slipping in the hand. In addition there were elaborately rouletted, round containers with lids, perhaps used for butter, cheese, or honey. The date of the output is not defined in detail on the site: but finds elsewhere show that it began well before the close of the second century A.D., and it certainly continued well into the fourth, though the figured vessels do not outlast the third century A.D.

The New Forest pottery is another and more restrained manufacture, whose period of production lasted from the later third century A.D. until the last quarter of the fourth. To judge from the types, the period of greatest output was in the first half of the fourth century A.D. This ware differs greatly from Castor ware. Its range of forms is much wider: flagons, dishes, bowls for table and kitchen, jars, cooking-pots, vases, goblets, and even candlesticks, appear in great quantity and certainly swamp the drinking-cups, though these also abound. Decoration, so far as it occurs at all, is restricted to very simplified running scrolls or conventional triangular patterns, all in white slip, and to repetitive stamped rosettes, demi-rosettes, or ogees. If Castor ware be thought the British counterpart of Rhenish pottery, the New Forest wares might be taken for the British version of vessels from the Marne or the Argonne. Their forms are shapely and sure, their decoration comparatively lifeless: Heywood Sumner, their excavator, observed that these works did not exhibit 'late-Celtic mastery of abstract line ornament, but fine perceptions of scale, spacing, emphasis, and restraint'. Though more varied, they did not range so far afield as the Castor ware. They were distributed throughout southern Britain but they have no place in the Midlands and the North, and never reached the military market.

Both the kilns and their output were less numerous; and the kilns, in small and isolated groups, were worked from huts so primitive as to suggest bothies and seasonal activity on a forest estate or public land. The impression created by this shifting, seasonal activity in the woodland is a little like that of charcoal-burning, and quite different from the old-established kiln-yards of the Castor potters' fields.

Apart from decorative wares, there was a vast output of kitchen wares and coarse table crockery indigenous to the province. As soon as the Roman armies arrived a profitable market was opened to such products, and the native potters were not slow to take advantage of the opportunity. At first they were content to supply vessels of their own type, though at once they improved the hardness of the pottery by using new technical processes. For some two generations wares of essentially Roman style and use, such as bowls for the table and kitchen mixing bowls, or mortaria, continued to be imported in bulk. Then they began to be copied. In four generations, by the middle of the second century A.D., the manufacture of common wares was entirely in provincial hands. The mixing bowls are stamped, in conformity with Roman practice, and, to judge from the stamps, most of the makers were natives, one or two of them endowed with Roman citizenship. The stamps attest a large number of makers; over sixty are known at Corbridge: but there was a big market to be supplied, over a long period, and many of the manufactories were small. How the commerce was conducted remains as yet obscure, but something is known of its ramifications. The northern military market, for example, was supplied by many northern potters, but Lincoln, Midlands, and even Middlesex potters took their share. Cooking-pots and jars, on the other hand, for which there was a much larger demand, were produced not only in small establishments but in very large ones, many of which are known by the wide distribution of their wares as opposed to the actual kilns. The extensive kiln-plants of Farnham (Surrey) supplied, with other unidentified establishments, the Thames valley market; but the Farnham wares have by no means the widest distribution of the comparable wares. The implication is that some vast potteries yet remain to be discovered. Sometimes, however, the military made their own vessels. The legionary kilns at the Holt, on the Dee, helped to supply the needs of the Twentieth Legion at Chester; the Ninth Legion, or part of it, was making pottery as well as tiles at Scalesceugh, near Carlisle; yet another legion seems to have manufactured attractive mica-dusted vessels for itself in the vicinity of Gloucester. At Ravenglass (Cumberland) and Grimscar, near Slack (Yorkshire), even auxiliary regiments made pottery. Yet these instances, interesting though they be, are in fact the exceptions which prove the rule, that the military market normally drew its supplies of pottery from the civilian trader. The picture evoked is as complex as that of Samian ware. There is seen an abundance of small men, concerned with a local market and sometimes venturing to bid for a military order. But there are also the great contractors, some tied to the military market, others serving chiefly the great centres of civilian population, yet able to take a large military contract in their stride. The variation can be expressed in examples. The potteries of Knapton and Crambeck both lie in east Yorkshire. Knapton cooking-pots are common in their home area, but do not stray far outside it. Crambeck wares are also well distributed in east Yorkshire, but they abound throughout the northern military area as well. An intermediate position is occu-

pied by Derbyshire ware and Dales ware, which fill the
farming settlements of the Pennine dales and reach also
Roman forts, but in much smaller quantity.

Legionary tileries have been incidentally mentioned,
but there were many civilian establishments as well. An
Imperial tilery existed near Calleva (Silchester) under
Nero. The *colonia* of Glevum (Gloucester) made its own
tiles, stamped *R(es) P(ublica) G(levensium)* and sometimes bearing abbreviated names of its *duoviri quinquennales* (see p. 90). In the same district there was a private
company, stamping with variant initials, much employed
at Corinium (Cirencester). More interesting still are the
stamped tiles from the villa of Ashtead (Surrey), which
have been traced all over south-eastern Britain as far as
Lincolnshire, Staffordshire, and Charterhouse on Mendip: many of the patterns are plain chevrons but there is
a spirited initialled scene of wolf-hound and stag at bay,
and some florid patterns with stiff but crowded conventional ornament, partly based upon ensigns of auxiliary
regiments. This establishment was working from about
A.D. 80 until after the middle of the second century A.D.,
and it is thought that it sent out journeymen to various
parts of the province. Another but much more localized
villa industry is that of Plaxtol (Kent), where the pattern
was formed by the statement '*parietalem Cabriabanus
fabricavit*' (Cabriabanus made this wall tile), repeated.

Reference has already been made to the dearth of good
stone for building and carving which obtains in south-
eastern Britain, and which led subsequent ages to rob
Roman monuments so thoroughly of their stonework,
ruining them in the process. In these circumstances the
good stone of the Jurassic belt became an important
article of commerce. Bath stone in particular was early
discovered and exploited. Colchester tombstones des-

troyed in the Boudiccan revolt of A.D. 60 were made of this choice freestone, a point which shows how quickly the Roman *negotiator* or concessionnaire turned to profit the natural resources of the province. But the export of Bath stone was not confined to the earlier period. It was being used in Weston-under-Penyard (Herefordshire), in the third-century gates at Silchester, at Lydney, and in London. Ketton stone was used at Verulamium, Barnack rag in London.

In Yorkshire the stone slates of the West Riding went right across the county, to Wensleydale and to the Wolds. Extensive use was made in the Plain of York of the local deposits of gypsum for manufacturing the liquid plaster poured into coffins to preserve the dead; the result being the remarkable impressions of corpses in their shrouds which are preserved in the Yorkshire Museum at York.

Quern-stones for grinding grain have been little studied. By the army they were at first imported from the Andernach lava deposits of the Rhineland. But this was not continued. Hard British stones, such as millstone grit and pudding-stone, were being exploited later, and an interesting field of study here invites an attention it has not yet received. Whetstones form a smaller yet important group. Large numbers were on sale in the *forum* at Viroconium (Wroxeter) when it was burnt down in the later second century A.D. and these are thought to have come from Northamptonshire.

Salt had already been extensively worked on the Essex coasts in the pre-Roman Iron Age, to which belong many of the so-called Red Hills, with their masses of broken burnt clay linings from evaporating furnaces used in boiling brine. The same process is attested for Roman times by its association with Roman pottery at Canewdon

(Essex), Goldhanger (Kent), Cooling (Kent), and Dymchurch (Sussex). But geographical sources also mention at least two places called Salinae, where salt springs and brine pits must be in question. The first of these is Droitwich, of which the brine baths are still famous. The Romans presumably used them for salt production, since Aquae, signifying a watering-place or spa, is not attached to the name. The second is at Middlewich in Cheshire, where lies the Roman site of Kinderton. A third Salinae, placed by the geographer Ptolemy in the canton of the Catuvellauni, remains unidentified: it is most easily explained as referring to saltings in the Wash, since no important salt spring is now known in their area. Finally, in the *Digest*, as Mr Eric Birley has noted, there may be a reference to *salinae*, or salt-works, worked by convict labour, in the military area of northern Britain; and he observes that the context suggests the Firth of Forth, where the name Prestonpans commemorates later activity of the same kind. These various places cannot have been the only sites at which so indispensable a commodity was produced, but there is no suggestion that the output went elsewhere than to markets within the province.

One aspect of British economic life which deserves attention is the use of water-power machinery. This was not a marked feature of Mediterranean civilization, since the chief necessity, a constant supply of water, was so often lacking. But it was from the Mediterranean world that the under-shot water-wheel described by Vitruvius was derived, and was used in aqueduct overflows for grinding flour and cinnabar at Rome, or for driving the Barbegal flour-mills near Arles in southern France. In north-western Europe steady streams were more common, and Ausonius describes mills for flour and for sawing stone on the River Ruwer in the Moselle valley. In Britain examples are few but significant. The army was driving flour-mills by water at three points on Hadrian's Wall, using for the purpose respectively the North Tyne and Irthing rivers and the Haltwhistle Burn. The stone core of the water-wheel's hub still exists at the North Tyne, and two hub-cores of the same kind have recently been found at Lincoln. At the villa of Woolaston Pill power-driven stones were re-used as flooring in a building close to an artificial water-leet; one occurs at the villa of Chedworth; while an iron spindle for similar stones from Great Chesterford (Essex) is in the Cambridge University Museum of Ethnology and Archaeology. The wide distribution of these relics is impressive.

The imports of Roman Britain remained no more static than the exports or the home-market. One of the oldest and most constant was wine, which, long before the occupation, was being imported on a fairly large scale by a limited number of tribal chiefs. Not only did they themselves esteem it, as the great storage-jars which fill their tombs declare, but the custom of lavish hospitality which it was a matter of prestige to indulge, demanded substantial stocks. At least it was drunk both lavishly and undiluted, with brutish consequences. When the conquest came the amount of wine imported must have risen sharply, since not only had a regular market been created in advance, but this market must have been on the increase. In addition, the troops, officials, and merchants who crowded into the new province brought with them a habitual taste for wine, which traders were ready to gratify. A coarse variety (*posca*) was an established part of the army ration. The only liquor which might rival it for consumption within the province was beer (*cervesa*), which in Britain, as in Gaul, was an esteemed drink, and unquestionably much cheaper. In Gaul, dark ale is mentioned as brewed in Trier (Augusta Trevirorum); nothing is known of varieties of brew in Britain, but a fourth-century panegyrist mentions the two-fold use of grain, for bread and for beer. Wine, however, must have been the drink on all occasions with pretensions to elegance or culture, and this preference must have been of great value to traders. How much first-class wine reached Britain remains uncertain.

The imported wine no doubt continued to be carried in amphorae. But it should be recalled that in the Moselle valley, where wine was plentifully produced and exported in the second and third centuries A.D., barrels were also used, and barrels of Pyrenees fir from Silchester and London no doubt contained wine from Gascony which the Italian consumer rated as second-class. It seems certain that Aurelius Lunaris, a rich merchant of Lincoln and York, who erected an altar in Bordeaux following a safe sea-passage from York in A.D. 237, was representative of traders engaged in this traffic and shipping direct to the northern market, both military and civilian. Lunaris was a Briton: but the same view might well be taken of the presence of a Biturigan, Verecundius Diogenes from the Bourges district, among the same class of merchants of York, since wine forms by far the most likely article of trade between the two regions, both then and now. It should be added that vines would seem to have been grown in southern Britain, vine-stocks being reported from a villa at Boxmoor, in Hertfordshire. Britain is also specifically mentioned as one of the provinces from which restriction upon vine-growing was lifted in the third century A.D. But there is no archaeological evidence for production: neither vats nor presses have been identified, and it seems clear that the climatic drawbacks must have worked against successful or constant ventures of the kind. Even if grown successfully, British grapes could seldom have been produced in the quantity or quality required for wine. It may be thought that such grapes as were produced were consumed as fruit, fresh or dried.

There was also a substantial import trade in olive oil, much used for cooking but perhaps even more for lighting; and the stamps upon the great jars, or amphorae, which contained it, come principally from the province of Baetica in southern Spain. This importation flourished chiefly in the first and second centuries A.D., and came to an abrupt stop following the wholesale Imperial confiscation of these estates because their owners had supported the British governor Albinus in his all but successful contest with Severus for the Empire. What took its place is not apparent, but the very large volume of the trade must have left a gap which required filling. Perhaps the olive yards of southern France or Morocco filled the gap. Certainly, whatever happened, the containers were now different and there is a very marked drop in the number of amphorae current. It may well be that candles, made in the province, may have taken a more prominent place as illuminants, while cooking fats, in which Britain must have been very rich, may have taken the place of oil for kitchen use.

If wine and oil were the principal imports for the table, its furnishings at first came almost entirely from overseas. The most costly and the most prized of table services were undoubtedly the silver jugs, dishes, and cups or goblets. These last were already being imported, if as rarities, in pre-Roman times. In the province, the silver plate which was the pride of every wealthy house in the Roman world came principally from the Mediterranean, though Gallic silversmiths were becoming important trade rivals. Some silver-ware must surely have been made in Britain, at such a centre as London. But surviving pieces follow classical models so closely that it is rarely possible to recognize a provincial copy. Silver-work which is certainly local, such as the silver decorative plaques from shrines or ritual furniture at Barkway and Stony Stratford, similarly follows the classical repertoire so faithfully as to lose much of the provincial character that it might have had. Only the choice of subject, as in the Capheaton *paterae*, enables a British piece to win recognition. Normally, then, it is difficult to identify British silver; and, while an East-Mediterranean origin must certainly be supposed for such a piece as the famous Corbridge *lanx*, a decorative tray which contains repeated references, both obvious and recondite, to Delos and its cults, it must be conceded that other vessels, especially those of the plainer sort, may have originated within the province. When potential craftsmanship is assessed the skill exhibited in beating, turning, and chasing the pewter table-services, which are patently British in origin, must be recognized and taken into account.

Bronze furnishings were also an important item in any list of imports. Among these figured elaborate table-lamps, candelabra, heated dishes, and containers, sets of strainers for wine, and finger-bowls. In the first century A.D. the bulk of these objects were indubitably imported, but gradually many of them came to be manufactured within the province; and there was an interesting half-way stage, during which Italian products were driven out of the market by Gallic merchandise. This is particularly noticeable in the bronze *paterae*, used by civilians for heating wine and food, and by the army as mess-tins, which came almost exclusively from Campanian firms in the first century A.D., but carry more and more names of

Gallic origin in the second. But details of British manufacture of metal bowls and dishes are also furnished by
the remarkable series of stone moulds of white lias from
Lansdown, near Bath. These exemplify not only the bowls
themselves but details of the handles, medallions, and
other ornamental features. The moulds seem to have
been intended for beating rather than casting and it is
not clear that the metallurgical work was done on the
spot.

In addition to bronze table furnishings, decorated
bronze work, both patterned and enamelled, poured in
from Gallia Belgica. The foremost place was taken by the
enamelled wine-ladles, cups, and jars; then came the rich
enamelled brooches and belt-plaques; and next the gay
bronze horse-trappings, for harness and saddle. Britain
had indeed its own enamelled jewellery, particularly
brooches; but these, lovely though they are, can hardly
vie with the best work from Belgica, which belongs to the
second and third centuries A.D. It is probably this, rather
than British work, that is meant by Heliodorus, who
assigns it to 'the barbarians who live on the borders of
the Ocean', a phrase as applicable to Belgium as to
Britain.

The Gallic capture of the Italian export trade in metal
vessels is evident sooner and to far greater extent in the
cheap ornamental table crockery known as Samian ware
or terra sigillata, the brilliant red glazed pottery made
both in plain vessels and in bowls covered externally with
moulded decorative scenes or conventional patterns. The
Italian centre of manufacture, at the height of its activity
at the opening of the Christian era, lay at Arretium, the
modern Arezzo, in Tuscany. Its products, decorated or
otherwise, were closely modelled upon the metal vessels,
of which they were intended to form a cheap copy in

baser material, and the owners were Italian merchants
working through slaves and freedmen. By the seventies of
the first century A.D. wares of similar fabric were being so
freely manufactured in Southern Gaul that they were
actually flooding the Italian market. Their decoration is
still classical in mode, though the figure themes become
coarser in finish and decidedly less ambitious in scope,
while conventional patterns acquire more flow and rest-
lessness. From Southern Gaul production passed at the
close of the first century A.D. to Central Gaul, and here
the decorative motifs, while normally still derived from
the classical repertoire, are used with still further freedom
and a new abandonment of restraint. It can fairly be
said that from now onwards, as the manufactories spread
from Central Gaul to East Gaul and the Moselle valley
(though Britain traded principally with Central Gaul),
the patterns are employed with increasing looseness, until
the jumbled scenes become little more than a patchwork.
The plain forms, too, gradually lose their sharp metallic
outlines and assume shapes more adapted to the wooden
forms upon which their moulds were made. Factories of
Samian ware hardly spread to Britain, where the illite-
bearing clay necessary for the manufacture is not found.
An East Gaulish manufacturer did, indeed, set up kilns
at Colchester, while moulds at York, Pulborough (Sussex),
and certain vessels from Aldgate (London) suggest tenta-
tive attempts to introduce the process. More interesting
perhaps are the native imitations of Samian decorated
bowls which copy their form and reduce their pattern to a
few simple strokes. These were current in the Midlands
during the late first and early second century A.D. But
British Samian ware was a drop in the ocean compared
with the vast quantities of imported Samian. The material
is so common as to be the bane of museum curators, but

to the archaeologist it is valuable indeed, since its ubiquity, its rapidly changing styles, its variety of makers' stamps, and its distinctive fabrics supply an unrivalled mass of datable material, often to be dated very closely indeed. The vast scale of importation may be gauged from the fact that no inhabited site in the province, whether farm, fort, village, or town, fails to yield Samian ware, often in great quantity. The army was certainly importing it in bulk, but how this traffic was organized and handled remains uncertain. For the civilian market it came in ship-loads, one of which, wrecked in the late second century A.D. near Whitstable (Kent), provided in later ages a name for Pudding Pan Rock.

Production of Samian ware was brought to an end by the invasion of Gaul in the later third century A.D. There was a revival of imitative fabrics in the Marne and Argonne regions in the fourth century A.D., with small conventional stamped patterns. In civilian areas of Britain this was widely imitated, particularly by the New Forest potteries. But it achieved a very considerable circulation in the south and comes as far north as York. In general, then, the gap was filled by now with various British decorated wares, but also by an increasing volume of imports of Rhenish glass-ware and Rhenish glazed pottery decorated with white slip. The glass jugs and decanters, bowls, and plates, are among the most attractive of Roman provincial manufactures; and while their elegant undecorated forms are pleasant indeed, there are remarkable decorative effects in cutting and twisting and astonishing figured works, of which the Bacchic dance from Dorchester, Dorset, and the Winthill hunt dish, now in the Ashmolean Museum, Oxford, are fine examples. The models and, it may well be, the manufacturers came from the East Mediterranean. Their fidelity to classical models is unfailing. This glass importation did not, indeed, begin from the Rhineland. East Mediterranean plain bowls, dishes, and flasks of lovely translucent glass were already being imported in the first and second centuries A.D. The most ambitious were the cups embossed with circus scenes. But a special and attractive group was formed by multicoloured, or *millefiori*, pillar-moulded bowls and jars from Alexandria, imitating the fabulously expensive murrhine vessels made of reinforced fluorspar. They no doubt appealed especially to the polychromatic colour-sense of the Celtic world. Neither in the earlier nor even in the later period, however, was the volume of glass imported ever equal to that of Samian ware, but there was much more of it than is commonly supposed, as a survey of collections at York and Corbridge reveals. It was also exported. Beyond the limits of the province, in northern Scotland, Roman glass of the third and fourth centuries A.D. is not unknown, usually in connexion with burials, though it must always be recalled that this reflects in a rich grave the conditions of life in the circle of the deceased. The complete Turriff jug or the fragmentary painted cups, from Airlie and Kingoldrum in Angus and from Westray in Orkney, may be cited as examples; and the last-named introduce yet another variety of late-Roman glass, which selects for its painted subjects the beasts of the arena. These also were made in the Rhineland, and so far as is known no elaborate glass was manufactured in Britain.

The Rhenish pottery, on the other hand, is in form such as might have been produced in Britain itself, and comprises jugs, beakers, and vases. The fabric is thin, with a highly polished dark colour coating, usually ornamented in simple running scrolls or medallions in white slip and also in barbotine. Sometimes the shoulder or belly of the vessel carries a terse, colloquial, and convivial inscription in white capital letters, such as '*suavis*' (delicious!), '*da mi*' (give it me!), '*misce mi*' (mix it me!), '*vivatis*' (long life to you!). The ware has a pleasant finish and attractive look. It is probably the kind mentioned in the famous inscription from the temple at Domburg in Walcheren, where a trader in pottery with Britain (*negotiator cretarius Britannicianus*) dedicated a statue of the local goddess Nehalennia 'for goods preserved in good order' (*ob merces recte conservatas*).

Lamps of earthenware were also largely imported, much from Italy in the later first century A.D. and thereafter from southern Gaul where the industry flourished.

Certain more exotic imports should also be mentioned. Mediterranean marbles were imported for use at Londinium (London), Camulodunum (Colchester), Calleva (Silchester), Corinium (Cirencester), Lindum (Lincoln), and even at forts in the far north such as Banna (Bewcastle). They include porphyry from Egypt at Colchester, Silchester, and Canterbury; Carrara from Italy on monuments or public buildings at Colchester, Richborough, London, Silchester, Cirencester, St Albans, and Lincoln; Pyrenean marble (*campon vert*) at Silchester; Peloponnesian marble (*verde antico*) at Bewcastle and also in the variety *rosso antico* at Lincoln; Euboean marble from Carystus (*cipollino*) at Cirencester. It would be wrong to overestimate the significance of such an item as marble, for the traffic can never have been large or even regular. But it is interesting to see how its use persisted and how the Mediterranean standards of culture adopted by the island demanded it. In the sixth century A.D. cultivated Britons still thought of themselves as *Romani* on the basis of language and literary tradition. But while the province existed there were many material links which might have justified the claim and this was one of them.

Another exotic import was papyrus from Egypt, which must have been in considerable demand, both by official bureaux, military and civil, for documents and by book-producers, whose skilled writers copied texts upon rolls.

Cinnabar (*minium*), which was an Imperial monopoly, was worked in Spain and treated in Rome. It was much used for painting the lettering of monumental inscriptions, in which traces of it are sometimes found. It represents another import which was rare but not negligible.

There was a limited but steady trade in cones of the stone pine for altar fuel and trade in incense must have been considerably larger. Cooking spices, notably pepper, ginger, and cinnamon, should be included: also perfumes in their glass phials, some from Imperial properties, such as the Judaean balsam groves, in their specially taxed containers, used by the living and for the dead.

No economic study of the province can be regarded as complete without reference to its coinage. A detailed study is here impossible, but there are some salient features which deserve emphasis. Britain seldom possessed an official mint. Only under the usurper-Emperors, Carausius (A.D. 287–93), Allectus (A.D. 293–6), and Magnus Maximus (A.D. 383–8), and during the years A.D. 296–324, under Constantius and Constantine I, was there such a mint on this side of the Channel. For supplies of coinage the province depended at first upon the Senatorial mint in Rome and the Imperial mint at Lugdunum (Lyons) and in the fourth century A.D. upon the mints of Treviri (Trèves), Lugdunum (Lyons), and Arelate (Arles). At the period of conquest a flourishing native coinage, normally of gold and silver, but in Essex also of bronze, was in existence and had been actively circulating for at least fifty years over an area extending from Kent to the Cotswolds and the Wash and overlapping into Yorkshire. A substantial number of Roman Republican *denarii* had also been imported and accepted as part of the regular currency. Once the province was created, however, it would seem that tribes or client-kings were not allowed to continue coining; not even one of the three client-rulers known to us appears to have issued any recognizable coins. The result was that in the native areas the ancient coinage had to serve as the medium of exchange, with an admixture of newly introduced Roman bronze pieces, silver being the principal money of account. This use of pre-Conquest issues died out in most areas at the close of the first century A.D., when a debasement of the silver coinage by Trajan was preceded by calling in as much of the pre-existent coinage as possible. But in the backwoods of south Hampshire and Dorset, native coins continued to circulate until about the middle of the second century A.D. From the first, Roman bronze coinage was widely welcomed; and there was a great demand for the bronze issues of Claudius, owing to the exiguity of pre-existing supplies and the immense influx of troops. Copies were therefore extensively made; the best of them in the legionary fortresses of the south-west and Gloucester, Wroxeter, and Lincoln, and were in A.D. 71 transferred with the Ninth Legion to York; the less skilled versions were associated with tribal capitals. Once the province settled down and new supplies increased the issues in circulation, the copying virtually ceased and the volume of Roman silver and bronze steadily grew until the middle of the second century A.D. Only gold remained rare and hoards of it are confined to the military area. A possible exception in the matter of copying is afforded by the *Britannia* issues of Antoninus Pius, of which some are so poor in quality that they may well be products of a provincial mint.

From the middle of the second century A.D. onwards, there is a marked decline in the volume of currency, whatever the cause, a drop which reaches its nadir about A.D. 235. Now also the conservative attitude of the provincials towards the coinage becomes apparent, in a preference for the old-fashioned purer *denarius* as against the new double *denarius* or *antoninianus* of reduced weight and impure metal of Caracalla and his successors. This is evinced not only by the composition of hoards of savings, but by the large number of moulds for illicit casting of *denarii* belonging to the period. Much worse was to come. The ruinous invasions of the later third century A.D. meant that already under Gallienus (A.D. 259–68) the central authorities no longer made any attempt to retain the silver content of the *antoninianus*; and the Gallic Empire, to which Britain adhered, won initial prestige by keeping to better standards. When the Gallic coinage in turn collapsed, Britain was flooded with base issues, hoarded perhaps in the hope of their redemption for something better. The new reformed issue of Aurelian (A.D. 270–5), Probus, and Carus did not reach the province in sufficient quantity to drive out the base coinage, and even when the usurper Carausius (A.D. 287–93) began his rule by issuing fine silver *denarii*, the Gallic coinage types remained so familiar that they were copied in the bronze *minimi*, issued locally as small change during the eighties and nineties. But the return to the silver *denarius* demonstrates yet again the monetary conservatism of the province, and only when Carausius received recognition from the central government did his two mints adopt the inferior Continental *antoninianus* of Diocletian and his colleagues, a policy continued by his supplanter Allectus (293–6).

The recovery of Britain by Constantius Caesar in A.D. 296 coincided with a new reform of the coinage, closely related to contemporary price controls, in which large bronze or silver-washed bronze coins (*folles*) were issued at high face value but in highly artificial relation to a gold standard. These new coins were welcomed, as representing a sound currency, and local issues of large copies were made in an attempt to resist reduction in their size. It is noteworthy that, whenever a return was later made to this size, even under the Gallic usurper Magnentius (A.D. 350–3), such coins were well received in Britain. At the same time the need for smaller denominations was still met by the continued circulation of the radiate Gallic issues, and by the issues of *minimi*, the minute copies of them. Constantius had one stationary mint in Britain, at London, and more than one travelling establishment. Constantine retained the London mint until A.D. 324, but his monetary policy was markedly different, since he brought the bronze coinage back to its metal value and drove out the over-tariffed heavy issues in an attempt to counteract the catastrophic rise in prices, which had been aided by the gap between the face value and real value of the coinage. The monetary history of the next forty years is in fact that of a fight between the two tendencies, the first to over-tariff the coinage and endeavour to fix prices, the second to bring the coinage back to real value and let prices find their level. The period was one of internal calm, only broken by the effects of the revolt of Magnentius (A.D. 350–3), which Britain joined, not without throwing up two minor usurpers, Carausius II and Genseris, who seem to have favoured the central government or hoped for recognition from it.

About A.D. 348, a tendency to restrict the volume of currency in circulation had become apparent, and subsisted until after the disasters of A.D. 367–9, when the new and profuse bronze coinage of Valentinian I, emitted by the mints of Arles and Lyons, began to spread widely over the province. A new phenomenon, too, is the silver coinage of Treviri (Trèves), which now became the principal silver-issuing mint of Gaul. No doubt this mint was supplied by silver from Gaul itself, but it is likely that the British lead-silver mines, worked by the *curiales*, also made an important contribution, which seems to have been paid for by the State in silver coinage. Britain at this period exhibits a wealth of silver and even gold coinage unexampled in any other western province. But the closing of all the Gallic mints in A.D. 395 meant an end both of this enterprise and of regular supplies of coinage, and it is the dearth of precisely-dated coinage after A.D. 395, except in the rare gold and silver issues, which makes the evidence for the numismatic history of the final phases of Roman and sub-Roman Britain, as reflected in the bronze coinage, difficult to interpret. The content of this late coinage is not in doubt. It comprises copies of third-century radiate type, of the coins of Constans and of those of the House of Theodosius. There are widely differing degrees of skill and style in the copies; and perhaps the most striking and dramatic feature is the reduction of size in some cases to 'minimissimi', coins so minute that fifty-one of them will cover a halfpenny. But it is now evident that all the striking degradations of style and module already appear virtually at the same time as the issues upon which they are based or from which they are cut. The determining factors for dating thus become such questions as relative wear and devolution of types, but, above all, the archaeological associations of the coins; and more material and study will be required before these can be decisively interpreted. On the other hand, it is of the highest importance to observe that the bulk of authentic Theodosian issues is so large in the area of the Home Counties as to suggest that active commercial enterprise, including close connexion with the Continent through Rutupiae (Richborough), was continuing until the third decade of the fifth century A.D. This continuity has been used to support the view of an official re-occupation of the province after A.D. 410; but it is in fact economic evidence, and does not illuminate the political scene. The continuing economic activity is further supported by the silver hoards of the worn and clipped *siliquae* which served as money of account in the absence of further new supplies. These fan out from the Home Counties to Somerset, Lancashire, and north Yorkshire and must indicate provincial communities still economically active until A.D. 420–30, whatever their political state may have been.

CHAPTER FIVE

RELIGIOUS CULTS

THE religions of Roman Britain divide into four categories; the official religion practised by Roman and provincial civilians, the cults native to the province, and the cults of the Roman army, official and otherwise.

One side of the official religion has earned considerable notoriety because it is enumerated by Tacitus among the causes of the Boudiccan revolt in A.D. 60: this is Emperor-worship. It is clear that the Roman government introduced in Britain, as in other western provinces, the worship of the Emperor to serve as a unifying focus of loyalty and of gratitude for the *pax Romana*. In Gaul an annual religious gathering replaced an annual tribal convention of Druidical origin, and the institution worked well; partly because it was continuing a tradition, if in new form, and partly because there was a large number of participant tribes, sixty-four in all, over which the cost could be spread. In Germany it worked less well; for it was not traditional, while the tribes concerned were much fewer in number. In Britain, most tribes had certainly paid dues to Druids, as the finds from Llyn Cerrig tell us, but their political rivalries must have made impossible any united council, and by A.D. 60 there cannot have been many more than ten tribes participating in the worship. These cults were costly. There was the central temple at Camulodunum (Colchester) to build and maintain, and excavations show that it was a large and sumptuous building upon which no expense was spared. It occupied a large court and in front of it there stood a

great altar, flanked by statue-bases, a design reminiscent
of the Gallic altar of Rome and Augustus, as shown on
coins. The British cult, however, was a personal cult of
the Emperor Claudius, to whom it accorded divinity during his lifetime with an emphasis which went well
beyond previous Roman practice. Claudius and his pleni-
potentiaries had been permitted to organize the province
without reference back to the Senate and this may be
recognized as one of the consequences. The observances
of any established Imperial cult were numerous and ran
in calendared order throughout the year. The tribal
aristocrats who undertook by election the priesthoods of
the cult for a year were accordingly expected not only to
reside at Camulodunum throughout their term of office
but to pay for festivals and games associated with the
honour but not part of provincial expenditure. 'In the
guise of religion the chosen priests poured out their whole
fortunes' is the Tacitean picture of their plight; and it is
not surprising that some Britons at least found the new
religion too heavy a strain upon purse and personality. It
represented altogether too sharp and burdensome a
transition into Roman state religion. After the rebellion,
in which the temple perished in flames, the cult was certainly established afresh. It has, however, been considered
doubtful whether it continued long at Colchester, in
view of the concentration of the government of both procurator and provincial legate in London. All analogy
would indeed suggest that the provincial worship will
have been associated with the provincial capital. Proof is
indeed wanting, but it may be regarded as likely that
about the end of the first century A.D. the provincial cult
moved to the administrative centre.

In the Roman *coloniae* or chartered towns, a temple in
honour of living and deceased members of the Imperial

House was an essential. The worship was undertaken by a statutory group of six priests, drawn from wealthy freedmen traders and sometimes from old-established citizen families, this being one of the duties which the community felt that new or rich citizens should bear. These men might be expected to give games or to pay for festivals, but also undertook less obvious but expensive benefactions, such as street repairs, bridges, or sewers. This Roman conception of the duty of a rich citizen makes it easier to understand the line taken with tribal notables, and in Roman society the idea was understood and taken for granted. Accordingly, the *Seviri Augustales*, six priests for the Imperial cult, appear both at Lincoln and at York; indeed, one wealthy trader was in A.D. 237 a *sevir Augustalis* of both cities. It is no doubt entirely due to chance that evidence for similar bodies has not yet appeared from Colchester or Gloucester.

The Imperial cult was an observance intended directly to promote the safety and welfare of the Roman state; and it was therefore a matter of immediate concern to communities of Roman citizens to see it regularly observed. From the provincials, of whom until A.D. 213 few were Roman citizens, what was required was an expression of loyalty. This was achieved, not merely by the annual public vows for the Emperor's safety, but by linking the worship of the Emperor's *numen*, or spiritual power, with public and private dedications. The process is well illustrated by the dedication of the temple of Neptune and Minerva at Noviomagus (Chichester), which the smiths' guild made 'for the welfare of the Divine House by the authority of Tiberius Claudius Cogidumnus, King and Imperial legate in Britain'. Here the famous client-king, whose loyalty was irreproachable, is securing that the foundation of a temple by a guild should voice their loyalty to the Emperor. A statue-base dedicated to Nero is also known from Chichester, and later still a second public religious monument was dedicated 'in honour of the Divine House'. The procedure may be compared with the dedication of a new theatre-stage in A.D. 138–61 by a magistrate of the *vicus Petuarensis*, the village-metropolis of the Parisi (p. 79), 'In honour of the Divine House of the Emperor Antoninus Pius and to the Imperial spirits'. The *numen Augusti* or *numina Augustorum* could thus be worshipped either by themselves or in association with other gods and nothing is more frequent throughout the province than this association of the Emperor's spirit with gods of every kind. An act of divine worship is thus coupled with an act of devotion to the Emperor, whose spiritual power and majesty is thereby enhanced. The frequency of the custom is a tribute to the readiness with which the province as a whole came presently to a loyal acceptance of Emperor-worship, despite an ill-omened start.

In addition to the worship of the Emperor, there was the worship of the State deities of Rome, in particular the Capitoline triad, Jupiter, Juno, and Minerva, not to mention Mars and Victory, Neptune, Apollo, Vulcan, Ceres, Mercury, and others. These were regularly worshipped in the *coloniae* of Roman citizens and in the capital, and this meant the creation of colonial and provincial *flamines*, or high-priests, who would be Roman citizens. At *Lindum colonia* there is a trace of corporate worship of both Apollo and Mercury by the different *vici* or wards of the town. Here also appear the Parcae, or Fates, worshipped by an official of a burial-club. A fine relief of Abundantia or a comparable personification introduces yet another typically Roman conception. There is also an elegant relief of a tutelary deity belonging to a quadrangular monument which might well be part of a column to Jupiter, of the type described below. At Camulodunum a statue of Victory is mentioned by Tacitus, and a fine head of Claudius is known. At Eburacum (York) literature similarly records a shrine of Bellona, the Goddess of War, and there is a noble head of Constantine as Caesar or newly-proclaimed Emperor.

As the provincials themselves became Roman citizens, all free-born becoming such in A.D. 213, the worship of Roman deities must have become still more widely diffused. There are signs of this in important provincial towns. Corinium (Cirencester) has yielded the base of a column to Iuppiter Optimus Maximus, restored by a fourth-century governor. Noviomagus (Chichester) has produced a similar and earlier dedication. This form of the cult is an interesting one, since it brings Britain into a North-West European circle of belief in a rider god who trod down the powers of the underworld under his feet and who early became identified with the Roman Iuppiter. Much earlier Minerva and Neptune had been adopted in the capital of Cogidumnus, as patron deities of the manufacture and sea-borne traffic of a guild of iron-workers.

But in the cantonal capitals an unadulterated acceptance of purely Roman cults is rare. The canton itself might be represented, as at Silchester, by a *Genius* or *Tutela* with mural crown. At Silchester also, there are traces of a cult of Mars, not necessarily a war-god in a Celtic environment. Hercules too appears, but only as equated with Segomo, undoubtedly a Celtic god. At Corinium Dobunnorum (Cirencester) the famous group of Matres, possibly the Suleviae, represents a cult of the Celtic mother-goddess, usually depicted in triplicate to indicate her power. The three goddesses sit stiff and

prim, as British as they can be. There was also a cult of
mother-goddesses with children at their feet, comparable
with the Nursing-goddesses (*nutrices*) of Pannonia or a
Trier mother-goddess and evidently a native form of
mother-cult, in Roman representational form. At
Verulamium, where the temples for the most part remain mute as to the deities worshipped in them, the
Mithraic token is one of the rare relics of a worshipper of Mithras in a cantonal capital, whether a
shrine existed there or not. At Wroxeter a temple of
Mediterranean form yielded fragments of life-sized
statues of a god or gods connected with horses, and a
remarkable piece of small-scale sculpture, depicting an
emblem of fertility driving a four-horse chariot, and no
doubt representing an aspect of the god there worshipped. In Isurium Brigantum (Aldborough) the tutelary deity of the canton, Brigantia, must have been worshipped, though the town has yet yielded no record of the
cult. Her statue, reproduced but hardly invented at
Birrens, is a remarkable personification, which combines
in one figure the conception of a territorial goddess, with
mural crown, a war-goddess clad like Minerva but with
an auxiliary regiment's type of helmet, a Victory with
wings, and a featureless monolith representing Caelestis.
Brigantia, whose cult is discussed further below (p. 198),
is elsewhere addressed as a water-goddess; but there is no
suggestion of a connexion with water in the Birrens figure,
nor is there any hint of the masculinity with which this
deity is once endowed in an inscription. Native belief must
have lain behind the conception, in part, but many of the
epithets and the entire translation of them into stone are
wholly Roman in idiom. Another native cult associated
with a northern native capital is represented by the ritual
bucket and sceptres crowned with busts of Mars which

went into the grave of a second-century dignitary of
Petuaria (Brough on Humber). At Venta Silurum
(Caerwent) one of the local deities, connected with a
guild, was Mars Ocelus Vellaunus, equated with the
Moselle valley god Mars Lenus. Mars Lenus was closely
connected with healing rather than with war, and it may
be presumed that Mars the 'Lofty' or 'Holy', which is the
meaning of Ocelus, and 'Superior', which is the meaning
of Vellaunus, was a deity of the same kind, whose activity
was not exclusively connected with war, however useful
it might be in wartime.

The deities of the native capitals merge imperceptibly
with those of the countryside, and so also do their buildings. The native type of temple, of which an early Iron-
Age example built in timber was discovered on the
site of London Airport, took in Britain and Gaul the
form of a high sanctuary surrounded by a portico
in which offerings or the god himself could be exhibited
and from which a large body of worshippers might be
addressed. The sanctuary was the dwelling of the god or
gods concerned and was not intended to hold a congrega-
tion. It was lighted from high windows above the surrounding portico, but these were sometimes small and
often open, serving essentially to light the shrine but not
to floodlight or to display its contents. In the Roman
province the form continued and had a long life, and the
same type of building was adapted to both round and
multangular plans. There is no need to think of these
modifications as due to Roman influence, and it may be
surmised that round prototypes at least will in time be
found: one has, indeed, been suspected at Maiden Castle.
Builders in the Roman manner were, however, able to
enlarge the scale of the building and to bring to its
embellishment many new materials. One of the pre-

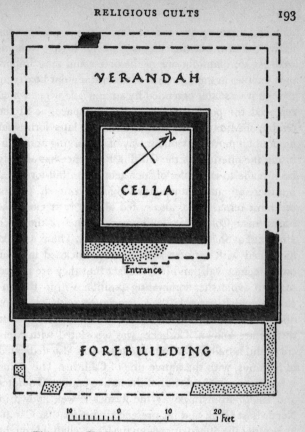

Figure 12. Harlow, the Romano-Celtic temple.

Roman customs had been to decorate such shrines with freshly severed human heads; 'a sickening sight till one got used to it' remarked a Greek traveller in Gaul. Carving and painting inspired by Roman architectural models would be an improvement upon this. Thus civilized, the type was widespread. At Silchester all the known

RB-13

temples, three square and one multangular, follow the native pattern, but their decoration was highly Romanized. At Verulamium one of the oldest and most important temples in the town was of the rectangular box-type, though it was later extended by adding side wings which replaced the portico. Such additional space, as at the temple of Mars Lenus, near Trier, in its later form, was no doubt a more convenient way of conserving and exhibiting the offerings of the faithful. Reference has already been made to examples of such temples in hill-fort sites, but there are many others in all kinds of contexts. One of the most remarkable, also noted above, is at Gosbecks Farm, near Colchester, while more shrines of the same kind exist at Sheepen, still nearer the town. These, as often happened with country shrines, were enclosed in their own precinct wall; and it is the fact that they are placed so as to avoid the dominating position within the enclosure which suggests their association with groves or open-air statues or the like. Dedications from Colchester shrines are known. Gosbecks was associated with Mercury, and a building nearer the town was also dedicated to Silvanus, with the native title of Callirius. This name is not known in Gaul, but of the native epithets Toutates and Alator from Barkway the former is well known in North-East Gaul, and his presence indicates that Camulos was not the only deity whom the Catuvellauni brought across with them. But there were connexions also with the outlands of the province, obscure though they be. Nodens at Lydney has his counterpart in Irish legend, Nuada of the Silver Hand; the sphere of Maponus, the native god of youth and music whose worship centres in northern Britain, seems to lie as much outside the province as in it; Mars Medocius Campesium was worshipped by a Caledonian at Colchester, and may be reckoned as

imported by him. Some deities were imported in Roman
times. Such were Mars Rigisamus from Aquitania, worshipped at West Coker (Somerset); and Mars Leucetius,
worshipped with Nemetona at Bath by a Gaul from the
Moselle valley, both being Rhineland deities. The Matres
also are thought to be imported, but if so they found a
very deep place in provincial affection.

Often, however, it is a local god or godling to whom
the shrine belongs. The highly complicated deity at
Maiden Castle, a Trinity of Bull, Female, and Owl, has
already been noted; Ancasta, the goddess of Bitterne; the
nameless goddess who broods ominous and hag-like on
the New Forest jar-cover from Linwood, published by
Professor Hawkes; Sulis Minerva, the splendid goddess
who presided with a sort of Pre-Raphaelite dignity over
the hot spring at Bath, or Arnemetia who performed the
same function at Buxton. The ritual crowns or head-
dresses associated with such shrines are also worth passing
note. Lydney yielded at least three fine ones, with scenes
from the cult-legends of Nodens upon them. The shrine
of Jupiter and Vulcan at Stony Stratford (Buckinghamshire) yielded an elaborate head-dress of chains and
plaques. A head-dress of the same kind was found at
Cavenham Heath (Suffolk), with another crown largely
stripped of its ornaments. It seems clear that many of the
small silver appliqué ornaments decorated with gods and
goddesses come from similar ritual vestments.

In northern Britain, where the military area has
yielded the bulk of Romano-British inscriptions, there
are a large number of shrines dedicated to local gods and
godlings: and these must in some sense serve as a pattern
for the many similar sanctuaries of which no record has
survived in the south. At Condercum (Benwell), on
Hadrian's Wall, the temple survives, a small building with

an apse at one end and a side doorway. Two fine altars flanked the apse, dedicated by commandants of the fort, specifying the godling here worshipped as Antenociticus or Anociticus respectively. His life-sized stone statue stood in the apse, but only fragments of limbs survive and a remarkable head which portrays a youthful god of wild aspect, with hair so thick and tousled as to suggest a bear-skin, and a torque about his neck. At Brocolitia (Carraw-burgh) the sacred spring of Conventina, which still bubbles up limpid in its stone tank, was covered by a temple of Celtic type in which the well or open basin took the place of a central shrine. Into the basin had been thrown not only offerings of money and knick-knacks, but eventually many of the altars and sculptured tablets from the temple. This happened early in the fifth century A.D. and so deliberately as to raise the question whether Christians were responsible. The sculptures illustrate Conventina sometimes as a gracious nymph, sometimes a single figure, sometimes raised to the power of three, but always reclining on a water-borne leaf. The offerings, nearly all bronze coins or pins and brooches, indicate a humble body of worshippers and the picture is completed by two home-made incense-burners, plainly the work of a votary who fashioned them and had them baked in a local kiln or oven. Three other local gods had a wider distribution. Maponus, who was worshipped at Rib-chester, Castlesteads, and Corbridge, was equated with Apollo Citharoedus, or Apollo the bard, who sang to the harp. His holy place, the Locus Maponi, lay north of Hadrian's Wall and has been identified with the Cloch-mabonstane, a megalithic circle on the north shore of the Solway which was in post-Roman times still the tra-ditional site for Border meetings. It was doubtless in his aspect of patron of peaceful festivities that Maponus found a place in the Roman pantheon. Cocidius, on the other hand, whose shrine, the Fanum Cocidi, also lay north of the Wall, was a god equated with Mars, and the silver plaques from Bewcastle which depict him show him in full armour with a spear of native type. His worship clusters thick in the basin of the Cumberland Irthing and to north of it. When it spreads out eastwards the god loses his identity as Mars and becomes equated with Silvanus, as if he were there the god of the wild. Once, too, he is given the name of another local deity, Vernostonus, at Ebchester. The identity of Cocidius as a war-god is not in doubt, and his name appears to mean, consonantly, 'the red one': it has nothing to do with the River Coquet. The third god is more exclusively Cumbrian, and his worshippers, to judge from their small and graceless altars, of humbler sort. This was Belatucadrus, who is also equated with Mars, but in the absence of a representation and in view of the lack of direct connexion with war which characterizes many of the Celtic deities thus equated, it will be wiser to suspend judgement as to his sphere of activity. Godlings there were in plenty. The local aspects of Silvanus, connected with hunting in the high Pennines, have already been noted (p. 143). Contrebis at Overborough (Lancashire); Mars Condatis at Piercebridge and Chester-le-Street (both Co. Durham), connected with a watersmeet at each; Verbeia, goddess of the Wharfe, at Olicana (Ilkley, Yorkshire); Setlocenia at Alauna (Maryport, Cumberland); Vanauns at Castlesteads (Cumberland). Some of these are river-gods, and on the Tyne Bridge at Pons Aelius (Newcastle upon Tyne), where the tides and the river met, Ocean and Neptune were worshipped together in a bridge-chapel.

Finally, there is the cult of Brigantia, of which the

distribution divides sharply into two regions. There are
the frontier dedications by troops or civilians, the former
occurring at Birrens (Dumfriesshire) and at Corbridge,
the latter in the Castlesteads area (Cumberland) and at
South Shields (Co. Durham). These dedications are
explicable as placating the *genius loci*, and a civilian
dedication in the same sense comes from Adel (Yorkshire). But the second group of dedications, from the
Calder basin, is erected by Roman citizen civilians, one
at least dating before the general extension of citizenship
in A.D. 213, who have the air of army veteran settlers.
If so, the dedications would represent shrines connected
with land settlement, honouring the patron goddess of
that particular countryside.

In southern Britain, many sumptuous shrines now lack
their dedications and there is left only the evidence of
devotion and a heavy capital outlay. The elaborate
octagonal temple at Weycock (Berkshire) or at Pagan's
Hill (Somerset) and the sanctuaries at Jordan's Hill
(Dorset) and Woodeaton (Oxfordshire) have not yet
afforded any precise indication of the deity worshipped
in them. The dearth of building stone in the most civilized
part of the island and the consequent robbing of Roman
stonework has affected knowledge of these matters regret-
tably. There are also the scattered objects, now divorced
from shrines, which have something to tell of individuals
and their beliefs. Such are the fine statuettes of Jupiter,
from Earith (Huntingdonshire) and Ranksborough Hill
(Rutland), or of the Emperor Nero, from Barking Hall
(Norfolk). The three richly decorated silver *paterae* from
Capheaton (Northumberland) depict scenes connected
with the army and commerce and with Hercules who
united them both. The gold and silver *patera* from Backworth (Northumberland) was given by a Roman citizen

to the Matres. The Mithraic figure from Whitton, Ipswich, recalls the imported Eastern cult associated with army or mercantile circles. The London marble statue of Oceanus is associated with a *mithraeum*; the London flagon which mentions a temple of Isis, commemorates another cult particularly associated with merchants from overseas and with shipping firms. The mosaic pavement of the Gnostic believer at Brading (Isle of Wight), or the Bacchic and Orphic pavements from Somerset point again, as noted above, to individual tastes and to those cults, which, like Christianity, set a standard of individual behaviour and salvation which was hard to follow but stimulating to possess. Of Christianity little survives. The written references to British bishops at the Councils of Arles (A.D. 314), Nicaea (A.D. 325), Sardica (A.D. 343), and Ariminum (A.D. 349) are supplemented archaeologically by the church at Calleva (Silchester) dated to after A.D. 360 and the remarkable Christian wall-paintings recovered from a rich man's villa at Lullingstone (Kent). The Christian mosaic from Frampton, or the hallowing by chrisms of a fountain at Chedworth seem also to indicate Christian families of villa owners. Christian finger-rings are possessions so personal as to be considered certain indicators of the religion of their owners, just as Christian formulae upon Cumberland or Westmorland tombstones suggest the same thing. But much of the evidence, consisting of the use of Christian emblems upon manufactured objects, proves little more than the existence of an atmosphere or climate not unfavourable to the religion which the Emperor had adopted. It may have little or no bearing upon the actual beliefs of the buyer. What remains indelibly impressive is the importance which the Church attached to the suppression of the British heresy of Pelagianism, and the fact that a well-attended con-

ference on the subject could be held at Verulamium
almost a generation after the Imperial government had
ceased to function in the province.

The civilian world had its regulated and calendared
observances, but these are obscured both by lack of direct
evidence and by the large number of private, sporadic,
and occasional dedications. The military world also displays an abundance of dedications of the latter class, but
there was so large a number of regiments, each with its
official cults, that the chance of survival is greater and the
picture so much the more complete. In Britain the class
of soldiery about whose worship there is least evidence is
that of the Roman citizen troops, the legionaries, quartered for most of the period of existence of the province at
the three great fortresses, Caerleon, Chester, and York.
Between them, these fortresses afford a fleeting glimpse
of official religion. A dedication to the legionary standards at Chester and the fragmentary door-posts of a subsidiary shrine in the administrative offices of the headquarters at Caerleon are almost all that remain of the
wealth of official dedications which such buildings elsewhere have produced in more favourable conditions. A
rich altar dedicated by a *tribunus militum* to the *genius
loci* for the safety and welfare of two Emperors in the
early third century A.D., a clerk's dedication to Minerva,
and a senior centurion's altar to Iuppiter Tanarus are the
outstanding individual dedications from Chester, and the
York fortress yields no better results. Only at sites where
legionaries are out-stationed do reflections of the cults of
their base-fortresses appear. At Corbridge (Northumberland), for example, the elaborate furnishings of a third-
century headquarters commemorate, first, the standard
of the detachment, with a decorative reference to the public festival of the Rosaliae, when the standards were

garlanded with roses for worship, and, secondly, the worship of Hercules, which was inextricably connected with the cult of the Emperor and the duties and labours of his army. These appear also statues of the Capitoline deities, a remarkable decorative panel and pediment from a shrine of Dea Roma, and also statues of the *genius* or guardian deity who presided over the individual unit or its station. At Newstead (Roxburghshire) a centurion commanding a detachment in garrison dedicates in the headquarters an altar to Iuppiter Optimus Maximus, the god who had so successfully guided the destiny of Rome for centuries. An out-stationed soldier on special duties at Dorchester (Oxfordshire) dedicated an altar and the screens round it to Iuppiter Optimus Maximus, reverenced in the office or post of which he had charge. The eagle of Jupiter crowned the legionary standard and so often crowned it with Victory. The goddess of Victory thus came to be associated with each legion and a silver arm, torn from a half-scale statue of the Victory of the Sixth Legion, demonstrates how costly and valuable the more portable offerings might be. Amid this array of official deities the Emperors had their due place, both on the decorative plaques of the standards and in the regimental shrine, where the statue of the reigning Emperor occupied a chief position.

The auxiliary regiments, recruited from non-Roman provincials, provide in Britain a wider field. Their regimental shrines did not house dedications to Jupiter, but contained altars to the guardian deity of the Emperor and of the regimental standards, or to the Emperor's Discipline, 'the Empire's strongest bond', as a Roman once called it. Most of them contained a life-sized bronze statue of the reigning Emperor, of which fragments have occasionally been found, as at Carvoran, or its great base,

as at Bewcastle (Cumberland). When Emperors multi-
plied, as in the fourth century A.D., their statues might
have to be placed at the approach to the sanctuary, as at
Risingham (Northumberland) or Brough by Bainbridge
(Yorkshire), or the shrine itself might be enlarged, as at
Corbridge (Northumberland). In addition there were the
standards to be housed, and in order that the chapels
might display effectively all that they contained, they
were often equipped with raised platforms (*suggestus*)
inside them and open fronts marked by low decorative
screens, behind which the holy things might be seen.

But if Jupiter found no place in the regimental shrine,
he and the appropriate associated deities had their recognized place upon the parade-ground, where the commandant of the regiment, acting on its behalf and in its
presence, took the annual vows for the welfare and safety
of the State on the 1st January and for the Empire and
Emperor two days later. Here, year in year out, new
altars to Iuppiter Optimus Maximus, the guardian deity
of the Roman State, were erected and the old ones
solemnly and reverently buried below ground. Few of
these buried groups of altars have been discovered, for
they left above ground even in Roman times no indication of their presence. But a remarkable group from
Alauna (Maryport, Cumberland) and chance finds at
Camboglanna (Birdoswald) belong to this category, and
such groups may well be there to find at every fort, if
chance permitted their recovery. The Maryport set,
though manifestly incomplete, forms an excellent representative example and deserves description. The most
numerous class is formed by dedications to Iuppiter
Optimus Maximus, plainly representing the annual vows
and offered both by the commandant personally and by
the unit corporately. Normally Jupiter holds the field

alone, but he is occasionally and significantly coupled
with the *numen Augusti* both by commandant and regiment, as also at other forts; and one commandant dedicated a building or, more probably, a *tribunal*, or
parade-ground platform, to Iuppiter Capitolinus for the
welfare of Antoninus Pius (A.D. 137–61). The repetition
of dedications and dedicators, related to the annual
renewal of vows, is frequent; five officers in particular
recur three or four times upon different stones, and the
units dedicating corporately are repeated many times
also. In addition to the altars of Jupiter, there are altars
to Mars, with the highly significant qualification of *mili-
taris*, to distinguish him from non-military types of this
god, such as have been already mentioned (p. 190).
Victoria Augusta, Imperial Victory, is another comple-
mentary dedication of which a duplicate is extant. Plainly
the series is incomplete, but it gives a highly interesting
and important picture of the annual ceremonies. A vivid
literary record of the same thing is furnished by the so-
called Feriale Duranum, a calendar of official festivals
(*feriae*) of the Twentieth Cohort of Palmyrenes from Dura
on the Euphrates, dated to soon after A.D. 225. The altars
belong to a special occasion, but the calendar reveals how
every week brought its own religious celebrations which
it was the duty of the regiment to observe and which
linked its traditions with the public worship of the Roman
state. That other festivals not covered by the surviving
portions of the Feriale were duly kept is shown by the
Derventio (Papcastle, Cumberland) dedication dated to
19 October, the Armilustrium. The third-century altar
from Borcovicium (Housesteads, Hadrian's Wall), set up
'to gods and goddesses according to the interpretation of
the oracle of the Clarian Apollo', is a particularly interesting special case, in which an oracular instruction was

implemented by Imperial order officially throughout the whole Empire.

The parade-grounds themselves leave little visible trace, except on hilly sites, where they happen to be deliberately cut and levelled; a fine example of this kind appears at Hardknott (Cumberland) and another at Tomen-y-mur (Merionethshire), while one at Maryport (Cumberland) was destroyed in the nineteenth century. All are, or were, large levelled areas, about 100 yards square, suitable either for squad drill or a general parade. Traces of a *tribunal* in the centre of one side have been noted at Hardknott and Maryport. They had their own deities, the Campestres, mother-goddesses in origin and no doubt imported into official religion by the Celtic regiments which even filled the drill-book with many of their own terms of command. The Campestres are normally associated with cavalry. At Condercum (Benwell, Northumberland) they are worshipped together with the *genius alae*. There must also be reckoned the deities disturbed by the reconstruction of a deserted fort, as at Newstead, where Diana and Silvanus, patrons of the wild who had taken temporary possession of the site, were honoured by the commandant of the new garrison. Sometimes an officer arriving in the new land would dedicate personally a whole series of altars to deities of local significance, as did Cocceius Firmus at Auchendavy on the Antonine Wall. Or such personal dedications might be made on completion of a term of office.

Within the fortress or fort most buildings had their presiding deity or genius. The commandant in his own house worshipped the *genius praetori* among the household gods (*lares*); and a Greek tablet at York mentions 'the gods of the governor's *praetorium*'. The military clerks, working in the unit's record-office, or the pay-clerks, in

the regimental bank, erected altars to Minerva. Each
of the *centuriae* into which an infantry regiment was
divided, or each *turma* of a cavalry unit, had its *genius*
presiding over the barrack-block, a deity sometimes
rendered in classical convention and sometimes descend-
ing to a comfortable everyday level. In the stables, Epona,
the goddess of ostlers, would find her place, as at Carvoran. The fort bath-house came within the purview of
Fortuna, not because games of chances were often played
there, but because naked man was particularly vulner-
able to the powers of evil and required protection. Sometimes this Fortune is called Augusta, sometimes Con-
servatrix, always with the intention of emphasizing her
power. At Birdoswald she is portrayed in person as a
statue, graciously enthroned, with her particular emblems
or attributes at her feet.

Outside the fort and beyond the range of the parade-
ground an auxiliary unit might worship collectively the
gods of its homeland, brought with it from overseas. At
Vinovia (Binchester, Co. Durham) the ala Vettonum,
from north-east Spain, was worshipping the *Matres
Ollototae sive transmarinae*, a useful if slightly inaccurate
interpretation of the Celtic word, which means 'of the
foreign folk'. A famous case is the Tungrians at Blatobul-
gium (Birrens, Dumfriesshire) who brought with them
their god Mercury and their goddesses Viradechthis and
Harimella. The Dea Hammia, imported by the Syrian
arches to Carvoran, is another case, matched by Virgo
Caelestis or Dea Syria, to whom a famous metrical hymn
was dedicated by the commandant of the fort. Mogons
was introduced from the Middle Rhine by the Vangiones
at Risingham (Northumberland), the Matres Alateivae
from the Lower Rhine by Gauls at Cramond (Midlothian). Apollo Anextlomarus from Eastern Gaul ap-

pears at South Shields and the Gallic god of victory, with his storks, at Chesterholm and Risingham. Another important introduction of the same kind was effected in northern Britain during the third century A.D., by the irregular levies from the Germanic fringes of the Empire. The Frisii from beyond the lower Rhine brought to Borcovicium (Housesteads, Northumberland) Mars Thinscus and his attendant female godlings, the Alaisiagae, four of whose names, each more outlandish than the last, are preserved. A second irregular unit, the *numerus Hnaudifridi*, called after its native chief, also participated in the cult. But whatever may be thought of the names of deities and dedicators, the barbarisms cease when representations are required. Thincsus emerges as Mars in armour, with attendant goose, while amorino-like figures with wreaths and palms, hover, like Victories, though, unlike Victory, they remain naked; similarly, the dedications are in Latin. The education in Roman ways and Roman equivalents has thus begun which will eventually turn these folk or their sons into Roman citizens. At Longovicium (Lanchester, Co. Durham) the Suebi were worshipping their goddess Garmangabis. The Germans at Voreda (Old Penrith, Cumberland) imported the Unseni Fersomari, perhaps the most uncouth-sounding group that has survived. This permission to outlanders to retain their homeland cults has sometimes been interpreted as a barbarization of Roman religion; but the *interpretatio Romana* by which barbaric cults were accepted, formulated, and shaped to Roman convention is no less important. So also is the frequent association of the dedications with the *numen Augusti*, stressing an Imperial loyalty. It was a Roman Empire and a Roman pantheon in which these deities took their place.

A more ambiguous northern cult, associated with both

the army and civilians, has left numerous dedications in the central and western areas of the zone of Hadrian's Wall. The name of the deity concerned is variously spelt and seems to have started as something like Hvitir; but it ends often as a plural, in the form Vitires or Vetires, so that, were it not for the ever inconsistent spelling, the dedicators might be thought to have intended their humble altars for the *di veteres*, 'the old gods'. Hvitir, with its initial aspirate, suggests a German origin and this is not forbidden by his equation at Netherby with Hercules or with Mogons. But to link the cult with German irregulars might be rash without further evidence.

Many of the western cults so far described were at a stage in which worship took the form of corporate vows rather than individual allegiances. The Eastern cults had a more developed basis of appeal and called for greater individual response. One of the most popular, especially in higher circles, was that of Iuppiter Dolichenus, the god of Doliche whose high seat was in Commagene, and who, with his consort Iuno Regina, made animal creation his footstool and the firmament of heaven his kingdom. He required for his worship a special form of temple, the Eastern house-type with many rooms, of which the existence in Britain is attested by various inscriptions. No British example has, however, yet been identified on the ground and excavated, although a fine sculptured frieze from such a building exists at Corbridge (Northumberland). His orders and advice were interpreted by the priest in charge of the temple, and it was no doubt his capacity to furnish responses to the perplexed that won for Dolichenus his popularity. To the army his appeal was also that of a powerful war-god and a great worker in iron for sinews of war. In Britain his worship first occurs in the middle of the second century A.D. but reaches its peak in the third. For a few years, indeed, the Emperor Alexander Severus (A.D. 222-35) and the Empress-Mother, Iulia Mamaea, were actually identified with Dolichenus and his consort, and worshipped in that guise in regimental headquarters, of which a relic seems to exist in a statue at Chesters (Northumberland). Less popular in the West was Iuppiter Heliopolitanus, whose mighty temple at Heliopolis (Baalbek) still proclaims the wealth and influence of the cult in the Syrian world to which it belonged. There is no doubt that the Roman world was disgusted by the zeal with which the Syrian-born Emperor Elagabalus (A.D. 218-22) plunged as high priest into the most extreme forms of Heliopolitan worship, and this is probably the reason why it failed to rival the less orgiastic cult of Dolichenus. Sometimes, on the other hand, the direct association of an Emperor with a cult seems to be the sole reason for its appearance in Britain. The connexion of Severus with Serapis is the likeliest explanation of the occurrence of a temple at York, and of a Kirkby Thore (Westmorland) dedication: it is certainly responsible for a Castlesteads gem, which shows him in this guise. A parallel case is the compliment to his Empress, Julia Domna, as Caelestis by the inclusion of this epithet, in word and representation, in the personification of Brigantia, described above (p. 191). On the other hand, it was a mistaken association with the Emperor Commodus and the public obliteration of his memory which led to the mutilation of a fine legionary dedication to Sol Invictus, the Unconquered Sun-god, at Corbridge (Northumberland) which had been set up in A.D. 162-3. This form of sun-worship also came from the East, but is rare in Britain, except when later associated with that of Mithras. Rarer still is the cult of the Tyrian

Hercules and Astarte his consort at Corbridge, with its altars (now in London and Carlisle) dedicated in Greek. This was served by a priestess, and is probably connected with the known presence here of Eastern traders.

None of these Eastern cults appears to have been so highly organized as that of Mithras, the god of Persian and Zoroastrian origin whose cult reached Rome in the first century B.C. Mithras was a god who exacted from the individual worshipper high standards of conduct, probity, and courage, in exchange for an ultimate revelation and union. Knowledge of the mysteries with their sacred symbolism, precepts, and ritual food and drink, was attained by grades of initiation, in which physical and psychological ordeals were included. For these reasons the cult was secret and it excluded women. It can be well understood how its tenets might appeal to a good soldier or an upright merchant; but to suppose that it had a wide appeal would be wrong. It asked too much effort, both spiritual and intellectual, in a religious climate where little was required. The suggestion conveyed by Rudyard Kipling, whose intuition so often enabled him to hit the mark, that Mithraism was a common religion, is belied both by the dedications and the size of Mithraic temples. The dedications are habitually made by officers and usually by commandants, while the temples in the military area are so small that they can never have held more than a dozen or at most a score of worshippers. The only temple yet known in the civilian area is the fine example in London, where a legionary veteran occurs among the wealthy merchant worshippers. Wherever they were erected, however, the temples always conformed to a standard type, in which the essential elements were the sanctuary, a long narrow nave flanked by single low solid benches facing out into it, and an outer room screened off from the nave. The heyday of the cult was undoubtedly the third and early fourth centuries A.D., and it is to this period that the excavated examples on Hadrian's Wall belong. Three are now known, at Borcovicium (Housesteads), Brocolitia (Carrawburgh), and Vindobala (Rudchester), the last being the largest, though the least well preserved. This is not the place for a detailed description, but interesting points emerge from comparison between the three. In the Rudchester and Carrawburgh temples the dedications were made by commandants of the regiment, who either introduced the cult or acted as its chief ministrants. At Housesteads the dedicators were a legionary centurion and a legionary seconded to special duties by the consular governor. It is evident that there was no long or regular succession of men capable of organizing the elaborate ritual, and both at Carrawburgh and at Housesteads there were indications of an intermittent use of the building divided by periods of abandonment, when it was deserted though in no sense desecrated. All three temples were partly destroyed by the barbarian invasion at the close of the third century A.D., but only Rudchester and Carrawburgh appear to have been rebuilt, while Housesteads remained devastated. The ultimate fate of Rudchester is not clear, but Carrawburgh was deliberately desecrated and thrown down fairly early in the fourth century A.D., its site being used henceforward as a rubbish dump for animal refuse. This looks like the work of a Christian commandant; for certain aspects of Mithraism, and especially the ritual meal, were regarded by Christians as a diabolical mockery of Christian sacraments. The different aspects of the cult should be noted. At Rudchester the accent in the dedications is upon the sun-god who was the companion and adviser of Mithras, except upon one altar, of which the sculptured reliefs refer to two of the different grades. At Carrawburgh the emphasis is upon Mithras. In one period of use stress was also placed upon initiation by ordeal, a cist for temporary entombment being provided. Revelation was later stressed and a remarkable altar depicts the god as he is described in an Egyptian liturgy at the moment of his manifestation in glory, his sun-ray crown being pierced for illumination from behind. Comparable use of a sudden lighting effect was made at Housesteads, where Mithras is given the title *saecularis* and is so portrayed, as Lord of Ages, in a pierced background of radiance enclosed by the signs of the Zodiac. It is possible that the different representational emphasis corresponds to differences in ritual, but in all the shrines Mithras and his two attendant gods of light and darkness are present, and at both Carrawburgh and Housesteads there is evidence for the existence of the central bull-killing relief, representing the conquest of wild nature by Mithras and his release of the vital forces from which sprang the good things of the earth. Whatever the variations in emphasis or presentation, it seems certain that the central tenets remained the same. One widespread misconception about the ritual should be removed. Although Mithras slew the bull to release the vital power of the blood, his worshippers neither bathed nor were baptized in it. There is no evidence whatever for this practice, which belonged to the worship not of Mithras but of Cybele.

So complicated a ritual and theology explains why the cult of Mithras appealed to few. Yet its personal appeal secured those few, and often influential, initiates at many points. In addition to the three known temples, there is evidence for Mithraism on or near the Wall at Castlesteads and Carlisle, Newcastle, Wallsend, and High Rochester, while the fortresses at York, Chester, and Caerleon have also yielded good evidence for local practice of the cult. The London *mithraeum*, with its numerous associated deities, is linked with Eastern merchants as well as with a veteran, perhaps associated with the garrison of the provincial capital, quartered in the north-west, or Cripplegate, corner of the Roman city.

Of other mystery religions there is little trace in military contexts, though Corbridge has yielded some fragments of sculpture suggestive of the worship of Cybele. Here, as in the cult of Hercules and Astarte, such dedications may be due to immigrant traders rather than to military men. Christianity has yielded no trace at all, though a Gnostic gem from a signet ring at Castlesteads may suggest the existence of a stray eclectic believer, just as there must have been stray Christians.

The religious life of the province was thus remarkably diverse, but from the Roman point of view there was rationality in the diversity. In Roman eyes the most important worship was that of the citizen body, corporately and individually. One of the reasons given for the extension of the citizenship in A.D. 213 was that there should thus be created more citizens to worship the gods, to whom the welfare and salvation of the State was due. While the evidence for regular calendared observances by Roman citizens in the British *coloniae* is weak, it is not absent; there is enough to make it quite certain that the requirements were regularly followed. The army, on the other hand, presents a remarkably orderly picture and its most remarkable side is not so much the Roman citizen army, of the legions, but the army of the auxiliary troops. While these men were not Roman citizens, they had nevertheless taken an oath of loyalty to Emperor and State, and their commandants were educated and wealthy Roman citizens. Such units worshipped the

Roman military gods corporately on the parade-ground and annual vows were paid both by the unit and by its commandant. But the matter did not end there: the military gods had their special festivals throughout the year, while members of the Imperial House, living and deified, were similarly honoured. All these feasts were duly and regularly observed, together with the more purely military functions, like the *Rosaliae signorum* or the Armilustrium. The troops could not take their part in such festivals without learning something of what they meant, either by observation or such actual instruction as might come from an intelligent commandant, with the effect that slowly but surely these conscripts from frontier lands learnt the import of Roman religion and felt their way towards conscious and responsible membership of the Roman state. Until A.D. 213, Roman citizenship was granted to them on retirement after their twenty-five years' service: after then, if they were born free within the Empire, it was theirs already and, although the old outward forms which distinguished the traditions of such regiments from those of the legions seem to have survived, they would take part in their traditional calendared festivals with a sense of still more immediate relevance.

The arrangements made for levies from the borders of the Empire, who supplemented the *auxilia* from the second century A.D. onwards, are less evident. It is clear that these troops were permitted to establish corporately their own native cults and that the dedications of such cults were usually coupled with vows to the *numen Augusti*. Roman loyalties were thus linked to memories of the homeland from the first. But it cannot be doubted that such troops also shared in at least the annual vows and the logical course would certainly have been to associate them, however distantly, with the general run of important festivals. They were destined ultimately to become citizens of the Empire and the sole question would be how rapidly understanding and sympathy in relation to its cults might be induced. It may well be that the first generation of men in such levies did not progress far beyond expressions of loyalty to the Imperial House. But in addition to this, it is important to observe how a Roman guise or interpretation is accorded to their native deities from the first, for this is in reality another and perhaps more subtle way of educating the worshipper.

Through the association of their own cults with an expression of reverence for the Emperor's *numen* the imported levies are in fact brought into line with natives of the province in general. It is clear that the opportunity for combining worship with a declaration of loyalty was regularly taken by provincials and it may be presumed that it was regularly expected of them. Otherwise there was evidently a wide diversity of cults, most of them harking back to pre-Roman days. It is difficult, however, to estimate whether such deities as the Matres were already indigenous to the province or whether they were introduced to Britain by Gauls from overseas during the Roman occupation. If these are eliminated, then the cults of the British province would appear to be considerably more localized than those of Gaul, or at least there is an absence of generally worshipped deities. This may well be true, for it would reflect the notable lack of political cohesion and cultural unity which permitted so rapid an acquisition of the province and defeated the first attempt to introduce a religious focus of loyalty at Camulodunum.

BIBLIOGRAPHY

This bibliography has been arranged chapter by chapter and in the order in which the subjects mentioned occur in each individual chapter.

LIST OF GENERAL WORKS UPON ROMAN BRITAIN

F. Haverfield, *The Romanization of Roman Britain* (4th edition, Oxford, 1923).

F. Haverfield and Sir George Macdonald, *The Roman Occupation of Britain* (Oxford, 1924).

R. G. Collingwood, *Roman Britain* (Oxford, 1924).

R. G. Collingwood, *The Archaeology of Roman Britain* (London, 1930).

Ian Richmond, *Roman Britain* (London, 1947).

E. Birley, *Roman Britain and the Roman Army* (Kendal, 1961).

A. R. Burn, *Agricola and Roman Britain* (London, 1953).

J. Ward, *Romano-British Buildings and Earthworks* (London, 1911).

A. L. F. Rivet, *Town and Country in Roman Britain* (London, 1958).

Ordnance Survey, *Map of Roman Britain* (3rd edition, 1956).

J. M. C. Toynbee, *Art in Roman Britain* (London, 1963).

CHAPTER I

MILITARY HISTORY

C. E. Stevens, 'Britain between the invasions (54 B.C.–A.D. 43)', *Aspects of Archaeology in Britain and beyond* (1951).

G. C. Brooke, 'The Distribution of Gaulish and British coins in Britain', *Antiquity*, vii (1933), 268–89.

D. Allen, 'The Belgic Dynasties of Britain and their coins', *Archaeologia*, xc (1944), 1–46.

C. F. C. Hawkes and M. R. Hull, 'Camulodunum', *Reports of the Research Committee of the Society of Antiquaries of London*, xiv (1947).

E. M. Clifford, *Bagendon: a Belgic oppidum* (Cambridge, 1961).

G. Webster, 'The Roman military advance under Ostorius Scapula', *Archaeological Journal*, cxv (1960), 49–98.

R. E. M. and T. V. Wheeler, 'Verulamium, a Belgic and two Roman cities', *Reports of the Research Committee of the Society of Antiquaries of London*, xi (1936).

C. F. C. Hawkes and G. C. Dunning. 'The Belgae of Gaul and Britain', *Archaeological Journal*, lxxxvii (1930), 150–335.

C. F. C. Hawkes, 'Hill-forts', *Antiquity* v (1931), 60–97.

J. P. Bushe-Fox, 'Fourth Report on the excavations of the Roman fort at Richborough, Kent', *Reports of the Research Committee of the Society of Antiquaries of London*, xvi (1949).

R. E. M. Wheeler, 'Maiden Castle, Dorset', *Reports of the Research Committee of the Society of Antiquaries of London*, xii (1943).

Hod Hill: O. G. S. Crawford and A. Keiller, *Wessex from the Air* (Oxford, 1928), 31–46; J. W. Brailsford, 'Hod Hill', vol. i, 'Antiquities . . . in the Durden Collection' (London, 1962).

C. F. C. Hawkes, 'Britons, Romans, and Saxons round Salisbury and in Cranborne Chase', *Archaeological Journal*, civ, 27–81.

Sir Cyril Fox, *A find of the Early Iron Age from Llyn Cerrig Bach, Anglesey* (Cardiff, Nat. Museum, 1946).

E. Birley, 'The epitaph of Iulius Classicianus', *Antiquaries Journal*, xvi (1936), 207–8.

Royal Commission on Historical Monuments (England), *Eburacum, Roman York* (H.M. Stationery Office, 1962).

P. Corder, 'The Defences of the Roman fort at Malton', *Roman Malton and District Report no. 2* (Yorkshire Archaeological Society).

I. A. Richmond and G. Webster, 'Excavations in Goss Street, Chester, 1948–9', *Journal of the Chester Archaeological Society*, xxxviii (1950), 1–38.

Legionary defences: G. Webster, *Journal of the Chester Archaeological Society*, xxxix (1952) 24–8, xl (1953) 1–24, xlii (1955) 45–7; also F. H. Thompson and F. W. Tobias, xliv (1957) 29–40: *Granaries*, D. F. Petch and F. H. Thompson, xlvi (1959) 33–60: *vicus*, F. H. Thompson, ibid. 63–8.

I. A. Richmond and J. McIntyre, 'The Roman camps at Rey Cross and Crackenthorpe', *Cumberland and Westmorland Antiquarian and Archaeological Society's Transactions*, N.S., xxxiv (1934), 50–61.

V. E. Nash-Williams, *The Roman frontier in Wales* (Cardiff, 1954).

Sir George Macdonald, 'The Agricolan occupation of North Britain', *Journal of Roman Studies*, ix (1919), 111–38.

S. N. Miller, 'The fifth campaign of Agricola', *Journal of Roman Studies*, xxxviii (1948), 15–19.

I. A. Richmond, 'Gnaeus Julius Agricola', *Journal of Roman Studies*, xxxiv (1944), 34–45.

J. Curle, *A Roman frontier-post and its people* (Glasgow, 1911).

I. A. Richmond, 'Excavations at the Roman fort of Newstead, 1947', *Proceedings of the Society of Antiquaries of Scotland*, lxxxiv (1950), 1–38.

Tassiesholm : Journal of Roman Studies, xli (1951), 123.

I. A. Richmond and J. K. St Joseph, 'The Roman fort at Glenlochar, Kirkcudbrightshire', *Transactions of the Dumfriesshire and Galloway Nat. Hist. and Ant. Soc.*, xxx (1953).

J. K. St Joseph, 'Air reconnaissance of North Britain', *Journal of Roman Studies*, xli (1951), 52–65.

Stracathro : ibid. li (1961), 123.

I. A. Richmond and J. McIntyre, 'The Agricolan fort at Fendoch', *Proceedings of the Society of Antiquaries of Scotland*, lxxiii (1939), 110–54.

Corbridge : see *Archaeologia Aeliana*, 4th series, vols. xi, xv, xvii, xxi, xxviii, xxx, xxxi, xxxiii, xxxvii.

J. Collingwood Bruce, *Handbook to the Roman Wall*, 11th edition (Newcastle upon Tyne, 1957).

E. Birley, *The Centenary Pilgrimage of Hadrian's Wall* (1949).

F. G. Simpson and I. A. Richmond, 'The Turf Wall of Hadrian, 1895–1935', *Journal of Roman Studies*, xxv (1934), 1–18.

I. A. Richmond, 'Hadrian's Wall, 1939–49', *Journal of Roman Studies*, xl (1950), 43–56.

E. Birley, *Research on Hadrian's Wall* (Kendal, 1961).

Sir George Macdonald, *The Antonine Wall in Scotland* (2nd edition, Oxford, 1934).

K. A. Steer, 'The Antonine Wall, 1934–1959', *Journal of Roman Studies*, l (1960), 84–93.

A. S. Robertson, 'The Antonine Wall', *Glasgow Archaeological Society Handbook* (Glasgow, 1960)

J. P. Gillam, 'Calpurnius Agricola and the northern frontier', *Trans. Architectural and Archaeological Society of Durham and Northumberland*, x (1953), 359–75.

S. N. Miller, 'Severus in Britain', *Cambridge Ancient History*, xii, 36–42.

Carpow legionary fortress : Journal of Roman Studies, lii (1962).

Cramond : ibid.

Sir Charles Oman, 'The First Forth Bridge', *Numismatic Chronicle*, ser. 5, xi (1931), 137–50.

I. A. Richmond, 'The Romans in Redesdale,' *Northumberland County History*, xv, 63–159.

Reculver : I. A. Richmond, *Antiquaries Journal*, xli (1961) 224–8.

J. P. Bushe-Fox, 'Some notes on Roman coast defences', *Journal of Roman Studies*, xxii (1932), 60–72.

W. Hornsby and J. D. Laverick, 'The Roman signal-station at Goldsborough, near Whitby, Yorks', *Archaeological Journal*, lxxxix (1933), 203–19; M. R. Hull, 'The pottery from the Roman signal-stations on the Yorkshire coast', ibid., 220–53.

P. H. Blair, *The origins of Northumbria* (Newcastle upon Tyne, 1948).

J. N. L. Myres, 'The Adventus Saxonum', *Aspects of Archaeology in Britain and beyond* (1951), 221–41.

CHAPTER 2

TOWNS AND URBAN CENTRES

A. Fox, *Roman Exeter* (Manchester Univ. Press, 1952).

S. S. Frere, 'Canterbury Excavations', *Antiquity*, xxiii (1949), 153–60; *Roman Canterbury, the city of Durovernum* (Canterbury, 1958).

J. S. Wacher, 'Cirencester, 1960' *Antiquaries Journal*, xli (1961), 63–71; xlii (1962), 1–14.

K. M. Kenyon, 'Excavations at the Jewry Wall site, Leicester', *Reports of the Research Committee of the Society of Antiquaries of London*, xv (1948).

R. E. M. and T. V. Wheeler, 'Verulamium, a Belgic and two Roman cities', *Reports of the Research Committee of the Society of Antiquaries of London*, xi (1936).

A. W. G. Lowther, 'Report on excavations at Verulamium in 1934', *Antiquaries Journal*, xvii (1937), 28–51.

S. S. Frere, 'Report on excavations at Verulamium', ibid., xxxvi (1956), 1–10; xxxvii (1957), 1–15; xxxviii (1958), 1–14; xxxix (1959), 1–18; xl (1960), 1–24; xli (1961), 72–85; xlii (1962).

K. M. Kenyon, 'The Roman theatre at Verulamium, St Albans,' *Archaeologia*, lxxxiv (1935), 213–61.

K. M. Richardson, 'Report on Excavations at Verulamium, Insula xvii, 1938', *Archaeologia*, xc (1944), 81–126.

M. R. Hull, 'Roman Colchester', *Research Reports of the Society of Antiquaries of London*, xx (1958).

I. A. Richmond, 'The four coloniae of Roman Britain', *Archaeological Journal*, ciii (1947), 57–84.

I. A. Richmond, 'The Roman city of Lincoln', *Archaeological Journal*, ciii (1947), 26–56.

R. E. M. Wheeler, *London in Roman times* (London Museum Catalogues, no. 3), London, 1930.

Royal Commission on Historical Monuments (England), An inventory of the historical monuments in London, iii, *Roman London*. (H.M. Stationery Office, 1928).

London, Roman fort at Cripplegate: R. L. S. Bruce-Mitford, *Recent Archaeological Excavations in Britain* (1956), 127–30; *Journal of Roman Studies*, xlvii (1957), 220.

G. C. Dunning, 'Two fires of Roman London,' *Antiquaries Journal*, xxv (1945), 48–77.

J. P. Bushe-Fox, 'Excavations on the site of the Roman town at Wroxeter, Shropshire, in 1912; 1913; 1914', *Reports of the Research Committee of the Society of Antiquaries of London*, nos. i, ii, and iv.

D. Atkinson, *Report on Excavations at Wroxeter (the Roman city of Viroconium) in the County of Salop, 1923–7* (Oxford, 1942).

Venta Icenorum: Journal of Roman Studies, xix (1929), 196; xxi (1931), 232–3; xxii (1932), 210; xxiv (1934), 209–10; xxv (1935), 213; xxvi (1936), 251; xxix (1939), 214.

V. E. Nash-Williams, 'The forum and basilica and public baths of the Roman town of Venta Silurum at Caerwent in Monmouthshire', *Bulletin of the Board of Celtic Studies*, xv (1953), 159–67.

Ministry of Works, *Caerwent Roman City, Monmouthshire* (H.M. Stationery Office, 1951).

P. Corder and I. A. Richmond, 'Petuaria', *Journal of British Archaeological Association*, Ser. 3, vii (1942), 1–30.

J. S. Wacher, 'Petuaria', *Antiquaries Journal*, xl (1960), 58–64.

Isurium Brigantum: J. L. N. Myres, K. A. Steer, and A. M. H. Chitty, *Yorkshire Archaeological Journal*, xl (1959), 1–77.

E. Birley, 'Housesteads, the civil settlement', *Archaeologia Aeliana*, 4th series, xii (1935), 205–46.

Air-photographs of vici at forts, *Journal of Roman Studies*, xli (1951), 53–5.

A. O. Curle, 'Description of the fortifications on Ruberslaw, Roxburghshire, and notices of Roman remains found there', *Proceedings of the Society of Antiquaries of Scotland*, xxxix (1905), 219–32.

K. A. Steer and R. W. Feachem, 'A Roman signal-station on Eildon Hill North, Roxburghshire', *Proceedings of the Society of Antiquaries of Scotland*, lxxxvi, 202–5.

Victoria County History, Hampshire, i, F. Haverfield, *Silchester*, 271–84; G. E. Fox and Sir W. H. St John Hope, *The Romano-British Town of Calleva Atrebatum, at Silchester*, 350–72.

M. A. Cotton, 'Excavations at Silchester, 1938–9', *Archaeologia*, xcii (1947), 121–67.

G. C. Boon, *Roman Silchester* (London, 1957).

F. Haverfield, 'Bath', *Victoria County History, Somerset*, i, 219–88.

W. H. Knowles, 'The Roman Baths at Bath', *Archaeologia*, lxxv (1924–5), 1–17.

F. Haverfield, 'Buxton', *Victoria County History, Derbyshire*, i, 222–7.

G. H. Jack and A. G. K. Hayter, *Excavations on the site of the Romano-British town of Magna, Kenchester, Herefordshire*, ii (1924–5); (The Woolhope Naturalists' Field Club): J. K. St Joseph, *Journal of*

Roman Studies, xliii (1953), pl. xiv, 1; F. G. Heys and M. J. Thomas, *Woolhope Club Transactions*, xxxv, 138; xxxvi, 100–16.

D. B. Harden, 'Alchester', *Victoria County History, Oxfordshire*, i, 281–8.

D. B. Harden, 'Dorchester on Thames', *Victoria County History, Oxfordshire*, i, 288–96.

A. H. A. Hogg and C. E. Stevens, 'The Defences of Roman Dorchester', *Oxoniensia*, ii (1937), 41–73.

C. D. Drew and K. C. Collingwood Selby, 'The Excavations at Colliton Park, Dorchester, 1937–8, 1938', *Dorset Natural History and Archaeological Society Journal*, lix, lx.

C. F. C. Hawkes, 'Roman Ancaster, Horncastle, and Caistor', *Archaeological Journal*, ciii (1947), 17–25; P. Rahtz, 'Caistor, Lincolnshire', *Antiquaries Journal*, xl (1960), 175–87.

Dorchester aqueduct: K. M. Richardson, 'Excavations at Poundbury, Dorchester, Dorset, 1939', *Antiquaries Journal*, xx (1940), 435–40.

Aesica Aqueduct: *Journal of Roman Studies*, xxxv (1945), 80.

Lincoln aqueduct: *Archaeological Journal*, cxi, 106–28.

Wroxeter aqueduct: *Shropshire Archaeological Society Transactions*, lvii, 133–7.

Sir George Macdonald, 'Note on some fragments of Imperial statues and of a statuette of victory', *Journal of Roman Studies*, xvi (1926), 1–16.

I. A. Richmond and J. M. C. Toynbee, 'The Temple of Sulis-Minerva at Bath', *Journal of Roman Studies*, xlv (1955), 97–105.

I. A. Richmond, 'An Imperial head of Constantine from York', *Antiquaries Journal*, xxiv (1944), 1–5.

B. H. St J. O'Neil, 'The Silchester region in the fifth and sixth centuries A.D.', *Antiquity*, xviii (1944), 113–22.

London Dykes: R. E. M. Wheeler, *London and the Saxons* (London Museum Catalogue, no. 3), 28: 'London and the Grim's ditches', *Antiquaries Journal*, xiv (1934), 254–63.

Public art and private wall-paintings: J. M. C. Toynbee, *Art in Roman Britain* (London, 1963).

CHAPTER 3

THE COUNTRYSIDE

B. Cunliffe, 'Excavations at Fishbourne, 1961', *Antiquaries Journal*, xlii (1962), 15–23.

H. E. O'Neil, 'The Roman villa at Park Street, near St Albans, Hertfordshire', *Archaeological Journal*, cii (1945), 21–110.

J. B. Ward Perkins, 'The Roman villa at Lockleys', *Antiquaries Journal*, xviii (1938), 339–76.

C. A. R. Radford, 'The Roman site at Catsgore, Somerton', *Proceedings of the Somersetshire Archaeological and Natural History Society*, xcvi (1951), 41–77.

Philip Corder and John L. Kirk, 'A Roman Villa at Langton, near Malton, E. Yorkshire', *Roman Malton and District Report no. 4* (1932).

C. A. Ralegh Radford, 'The Roman villa at Ditchley, Oxon', *Oxoniensia*, i (1936), 24–69; *Victoria County History, Oxfordshire*, i, 311–12.

Little Milton: *Journal of Roman Studies*, xl (1950), pp. vi, 2.

Clanville: *Victoria County History, Hampshire and the Isle of Wight*, 295–7; *Archaeologia*, lvi (1898), 2–6.

Denton: *Journal of Roman Studies*, xl (1950), 100; William Fowler, *Engravings of the principal Mosaic Pavements which have been discovered . . . in various parts of Great Britain, etc.* (1804), pls. 9, 10.

Castlefield: *Victoria County History, Hampshire*, i, 302.

S. E. Winbolt, *Roman Folkestone* (1925); *Victoria County History, Kent*, iii, 114–15.

Samuel Lysons, *Roman Antiquities at Woodchester* (1797); *Reliquiae Britannico-Romanae*, ii (1813), part i.

Northleigh: *Victoria County History, Oxfordshire*, i, 316–18.

V. E. Nash-Williams, 'The Roman Villa at Llantwit Major in Glamorgan', *Archaeologia Cambrensis*, cii (1953), 89–163.

Chedworth: *National Trust Guide*, 1962.

Titsey: G. E. Fox, *Archaeologia*, lix (1905), 214–18.

Darenth: ibid., 218–31; G. Payne, 'The Roman Villa at Darenth', *Archaeologia Cantiana*, xxii (1896), 49–84; *Victoria County History, Kent*, iii, 111–13.

A. H. Cocks, 'A Romano-British Homestead in the Hambleden Valley, Bucks', *Archaeologia*, lxxi (1921), 140–98.

A. M. Woodward, 'The Roman Villa at Rudston, Yorkshire', *Archaeological Journal*, xxxi (1934), 366–76; xxxii (1936), 214–20; with K. A. Steer, xxxiii (1938), 81–6; K. A. Steer, ibid., 321–38.

I. A. Richmond, T. Romans, R. P. Wright, 'A civilian Bath-house of the Roman Period at Old Durham, *Archaeologia Aeliana*, 4th series, xxii (1944), 1–21; R. P. Wright and J. P. Gillam, 'Second Report on Roman Buildings at Old Durham', ibid., xxix (1951), 203–12; 'Third Report', ibid., xxxi (1953), 116–26.

Professor Buckman and C. H. Newmarch, *Remains of Roman Art in Cirencester . . . ancient Corinium* (London, 1850).

A. Fox, 'The date of the Orpheus mosaic', *Transactions of the Bristol and Gloucester Archaeological Society*, lxx (1951), 51–3.

H. Eckroyd Smith, *Reliquiae Isurianae* (1852); *A Roman Mosaic Pavement* (1867).

I. A. Richmond, *The Roman Pavements at Rudston*, 1935.

Lenthay Green mosaic: Royal Commission on Historical Monuments (England), *Report on West Dorset* (1952), 199, pl. 127.

Low Ham mosaic: Somerset Arch. and Nat. Hist. Soc. Proceedings, xcii (1946), 25–8; *Journal of Roman Studies*, xxxvi (1946), 142, pl. xi.

B. W. Pearce, 'Roman Site at Otford', *Archaeologia Cantiana*, xxxix (1927), 153; *Victoria County History*, Kent, iii, 122; *Journal of Roman Studies*, xvi (1926).

G. W. Meates, *Lullingstone Roman Villa* (London, 1955); also *Lullingstone Roman Villa* (Guide, H.M. Stationery Office, 1962).

J. E. and F. G. Hilton Price, *Remains of Roman Buildings at Morton near Brading* (London, 1887); *Victoria County History, Hampshire and the Isle of Wight*, i, 313–16.

Victoria County History, Leicestershire, i, 188–97.

Bramdean Mosaic: Victoria County History, Hampshire and the Isle of Wight, i, 307–8.

William Fowler, *Engravings of the principal Mosaic Pavements which have been discovered . . . in various parts of Great Britain, etc.* (1804), pl. 2.

R. Hinks, *Catalogue of the Greek, Etruscan, and Roman Paintings and Mosaics in the British Museum* (1933), 101–2, no. 36a–p.

Gosbecks: M. R. Hull, 'Roman Colchester', *Reports of the Research Committee of the Society of Antiquaries of London*, xx (1958), 259–71.

Woodeaton: M. V. Taylor, *Victoria County History, Oxfordshire*, i, 299–301; J. R. Kirk, *Oxoniensia*, xiv (1949), 1–45; R. Goodchild and J. R. Kirk, ibid., xix (1954), 15–37.

loca: I. A. Richmond and O. G. S. Crawford, 'The British section of the Ravenna Cosmography', *Archaeologia*, xciii, 15.

R. E. M. and T. V. Wheeler, 'Report on the excavation of the Prehistoric, Roman, and post-Roman site in Lydney Park, Gloucestershire, *Reports of the Research Committee of the Society of Antiquaries of London*, ix (1932).

C. E. Stevens, 'A possible conflict of laws in Roman Britain', *Journal of Roman Studies*, xxxvii (1947), 132–4.

C. F. C. Hawkes, 'Britons, Romans, and Saxons round Salisbury and in Cranborne Chase', *Archaeological Journal*, civ (1948), 1–48.

F. C. Payne, 'The plough in ancient Britain', *Archaeological Journal*, civ, 82–111.

F. Haverfield, 'Centuriation in Roman Essex', *Essex Archaeological Society Transactions*, xv (1921), 115–25.

J. G. D. Clark, 'Report on excavations on the Cambridgeshire Car Dyke, 1947', *Antiquaries Journal*, xxix (1949), 145–63.

Villages: Royal Commission on Historical Monuments (England), *An Inventory of the historical monuments in Westmorland*, p. xxxii ff. (1936).

R. G. Collingwood, 'Prehistoric settlements near Crosby Ravensworth', *Cumberland and Westmorland Antiquarian and Archaeological Society's Trans.*, N.S. xxxiii (1933), 201–26.

A. Raistrick, 'Iron-Age settlements in West Yorkshire', *Yorkshire Archaeological Journal*, xxxiv (1939), 115–50; *Journal of Roman Studies*, xl (1950), pl. vi, 1.

Gargrave: R. Rauthmel, *Antiquitates Bremetonacenses or The Roman Antiquities of Overborough* (2nd edition, Kirby Lonsdale, 1824), 16–17.

I. A. Richmond, 'The Sarmatae, Bremetennacum Veteranorum and the regio Bremetennacensis', *Journal of Roman Studies*, xxxv (1945), 15–29.

Lake-dwellings: V. G. Childe, *The Prehistory of Scotland*, 211–12.

R. E. M. Wheeler, 'A Romano-Celtic temple near Harlow, Essex, and a note on the type', *Antiquaries Journal*, viii (1928), 300–26.

J. S. P. Bradford and R. G. Goodchild, 'Excavations at Frilford, Berkshire, 1937–8', *Oxoniensia*, iii, 1–70.

Titsey Temple: *Journal of Roman Studies*, xxvi (1936), 262–3.

Nettleton Shrub: F. Haverfield, *Roman Britain in 1913* (British Academy Supplemental Papers, ii), 49.

Barkway: British Museum: *Guide to the Antiquities of Roman Britain in the Department of British and Medieval Antiquities*, 34–6; *Victoria County History, Hertfordshire*, iv (1914), 149, pl. x.

Stony Stratford: British Museum: *Guide to the Antiquities of Roman Britain in the Department of British and Medieval Antiquities* (1922), 36.

Ialonus: *Transactions of the Historic Society of Lancashire and Cheshire*, cv (1953), 18–23.

Vinotonus: *Journal of Roman Studies*, xxxvi (1946), 146; xxxvii (1947), 179.

G. C. Dunning and R. F. Jessup, 'Roman Barrows', *Antiquity*, x (1936), 37–53.

J. P. Gillam and C. M. Daniels, 'The Roman mausoleum on Shorden Brae, Corbridge', *Archaeologia Aeliana*, ser. 4, xxxix (1961), 37–61.

Walled cemeteries: *Victoria County History, Kent*, iii, 94, pl. xiv.

Mersea: Royal Commission on Historical Monuments (England), *Essex (North-East)*, 229–30.

Harpenden: St Albans and Hertfordshire Architectural and Archaeological Society Transactions (1937), 108–14.

J. P. Bushe-Fox, 'Fourth Report on the Excavations of the Roman
    fort at Richborough, Kent'; *Reports of the Research Committee of
    the Society of Antiquaries of London*, xvi (1949), 38–48.

I. A. Richmond and R. P. Wright, 'Stones from a Hadrianic war
    memorial on Tyneside', *Archaeologia Aeliana*, 4th series, xxi, 93–
    120.

Hawkshaw head: J. Curle, 'An inventory of objects of Roman and pro-
    vincial Roman origin found on sites in Scotland not definitely
    associated with Roman constructions', *Proceedings of the Society of
    Antiquaries of Scotland*, lxvi (1931–2), 326–9.

CHAPTER 4

ECONOMICS

R. G. Collingwood, 'Roman Britain', in *An Economic Survey of Ancient
    Rome*, iii, 1–118.

R. G. Collingwood, 'Roman Britain', chapter iv, *Mining and minerals*,
    An Economic Survey of Ancient Rome, iii.

O. Davies, *Roman mines in Europe* (Oxford, 1935); *The British Isles*,
    140–64.

G. C. Whittick, 'Roman mining in Britain', *Transactions of the
    Newcomen Society*, xii (1931–2), 57–79.

R. F. Tylecote, *Metallurgy in Archaeology* (London, 1962).

J. A. Smythe, 'Roman pigs of lead from Brough', *Transactions of the
    Newcomen Society*, xx (1939–40), 139–45.

I. A. Richmond, 'Roman leaden sealings from Brough-under-
    Stainmore', *Cumberland and Westmorland Antiquarian and Archaeo-
    logical Society Transactions*, N.S., xxxvi (1936), 104–25.

J. A. Smythe, 'Roman objects of copper and iron from the north of
    England', *Proceedings of the University of Durham Philosophical
    Society*, ix (1938), Appendix, *Paraffin wax*, 400–1.

Machen: V. E. Nash-Williams, *Archaeologia Cambrensis*, xciv (1939),
    108.

O. Davies, 'The copper mines on Great Orme's Head, Caernarvon-
    shire', *Archaeologia Cambrensis*, c (1948), 61–6.

Anglesey copper: Royal Commission on Ancient Monuments, Wales,
    Anglesey, Appendices III and IV, pp. lxxxvi-xc.

V. E. Nash-Williams, 'The Roman gold-mines at Dolaucothi
    (Carm.)', *Bulletin of the Board of Celtic Studies*, xiv (1950), 79–84;
    aqueduct, G. D. B. Jones, I. J. Blakey and E. C. F. Macpherson,
    ibid. xix, 71–84.

Water-lifting wheels: O. Davies, *Archaeologia Cambrensis*, xci (1936), 51–7.

Corbridge iron-working: Archaeologia Aeliana, 3rd series, viii, 207–9.

Coal: R. G. Collingwood, *Economic Survey of Ancient Rome*, iii, 35–7; also G. Webster, *Antiquaries Journal*, xxxv (1955), 199–217.

Kimmeridge shale: British Museum Guide to the Antiquities of Roman Britain (1922), 69–71; *Journal of Roman Studies*, xxii (1932), 206–7.

Purbeck Marble: G. C. Dunning, *Archaeological News-letter*, March 1949, 15.

Jet and gypsum: I. A. Richmond, 'The four *coloniae* of Roman Britain', *Archaeological Journal*, ciii (1947), 79.

M. Steuart, 'Scots pearls', *Scottish Historical Review*, xvii (1920), 287–95.

Birri and *tapetia:* G. Caputo and R. Goodchild, 'Diocletian's price-edict at Ptolemais (Cyrenaica)', *Journal of Roman Studies*, xlv (1955), 106–15.

Cropping shears: Archaeological Journal, xiii, 10, pl. 3, no. 30.

Dye-works: Silchester, *Archaeologia*, liv, 459–67; *Victoria County History, Hampshire*, i, 353.

E. T. Artis, *The Durobrivae of Antoninus, etc.*, London, 1828.

Heywood Sumner, *New Forest Pottery Sites* (1927).

H. M. Callender, 'Amphora stamps from Corbridge', *Archaeologia Aeliana*, 4th series, xxvii (1949), 60–117.

A. W. G. Lowther, *A survey of the prehistory of the Farnham district*, part iii (Surrey Archaeological Society, 1939), 221 ff.

W. F. Grimes, 'Pottery and Tilery of the XXth Legion at Holt', *Cymmrodorion Society Transactions* (1930).

Knapton pottery: P. Corder and J. L. Kirk, 'The Roman villa at Langton', *Roman Malton and District Report, no. 3*, 96.

P. Corder, 'The Roman pottery at Crambeck, Castle Howard', *Roman Malton and District Report no. 1* (1928).

P. Corder, 'A pair of fourth-century Romano-British pottery kilns near Crambeck, with a note on the distribution of Crambeck ware, by Margaret Birley', *Antiquaries Journal*, xvii (1937), 392–413.

J. P. Gillam, 'Roman-British Derbyshire ware', *Antiquaries Journal*, xix (1939), 429–37; 'Dales Ware', ibid., xxxi (1951), 154–64.

A. W. G. Lowther, 'A Study of the patterns on Roman flue-tiles and their distribution', *Research papers of the Surrey Archaeological Society*, no. 1 (1948).

Plaxtol tiles: F. Haverfield, *Proceedings of the Society of Antiquaries of London*, xxiii (1911), 109.

I. A. Richmond, 'Part of the stem of a Roman monumental candela-brum of stone, from York', *Antiquaries Journal*, xxvi (1946), 1–10.

Capheaton paterae: British Museum Guide to the Antiquities of Roman Britain (1922), 90–3.

R. C. Bosanquet, 'A Roman skillet from South Shields', *Archaeologia Aeliana*, 4th series, xiii (1936), 139–51.

Colchester Samian pottery: M. R. Hull, *Germania*, xviii (1934), 27–36.

G. Simpson, 'The Aldgate potter, a maker of Romano-British Samian ware', *Journal of Roman Studies*, xlii (1952), 68–71.

Glass: I. A. Richmond, 'The four *coloniae* of Roman Britain', *Archaeological Journal*, ciii (1947), 80.

Marble imported: Journal of Roman Studies, xii (1922), 221.

C. H. V. Sutherland, *Coinage and currency in Roman Britain* (Oxford, 1937).

C. H. V. Sutherland, 'Romano-British imitations of bronze coins of Claudius I', *Numismatic Notes and Monographs*, no. 65 (New York, 1935).

B. H. St J. O'Neil, 'A hoard of late Roman coins from Northampton-shire; its parallels and significance', *Archaeological Journal*, xc, 282–305.

G. C. Boon, 'The Roman temple at Brean Down, Somerset, and the dating of "Minimissimi"', *Numismatic Chronicle*, 1961 (1962), 191–7.

CHAPTER 5

RELIGIONS

Colchester: M. R. Hull, 'Roman Colchester', *Reports of the Research Committee of the Society of Antiquaries of London*, xx (1958), 162–91.

Jupiter-column: F. Haverfield, *Archaeologia*, lxix (1920), 188–91.

Chichester inscription: Tacitus, *Agricola*, Furneaux and Anderson (Oxford, 1922), 79, fig. 10.

Silchester Tutela: Victoria County History, Hampshire, i, 363.

Segomo: Victoria County History, Hampshire, i, 280, fig. 7.

Matres: F. Haverfield, *Archaeologia*, lxix (1920), 181.

Nutrices: Archaeologia, lxix (1920), 183–4.

Cybele: R. E. M. and T. V. Wheeler, 'Verulamium, a Belgic and two Roman cities', *Reports of the Research Committee of the Society of Antiquaries of London*, xi (1936), 113–20.

Brigantia: N. Joliffe, *Archaeological Journal*, xcviii (1941), 36–61.

P. Corder and I. A. Richmond, 'A Romano-British interment, with bucket and sceptres, from Brough, East Yorkshire', *Antiquaries Journal*, xviii (1938), 68–74.

Ocelus: V. E. Nash-Williams, *Bulletin of the Board of Celtic Studies*, xv (1951), 90–3.

Silchester temple: Archaeologia, liv, 206–9.

Verulamium temple: Antiquaries Journal, xvii (1937), 28–51.

Gosbecks temple-site: M. R. Hull, 'Roman Colchester', *Reports of the Research Committee of the Society of Antiquaries of London*, xx (1958), 259–71.

Gosbecks Mercury: ibid.; also *Journal of Roman Studies*, xxxviii (1948), pl. xiv.

Mars Medocius: Archaeological Journal, xlix, 215–19.

Rigisamus: R. G. Collingwood, *Proceedings of the Somersetshire Archaeological and Natural History Society*, lxxvii (1931), 112–14.

Leucetius: Victoria County History, Somerset, i, 272.

R. E. M. Wheeler, 'Maiden Castle, Dorset', *Reports of the Research Committee of the Society of Antiquaries of London*, xii (1943), 131–4.

Ancasta: Victoria County History, Hampshire, i, 336.

N. F. Layard, 'Bronze crowns and a bronze head-dress from a Roman site on Cavenham Heath, Suffolk', *Antiquaries Journal*, v (1925), 258–65.

Antenociticus: I. A. Richmond, *Archaeologia Aeliana*, 4th series, xix (1941), 37–9.

Coventina: Archaeologia Aeliana, 2nd series, viii (1880), 1–49.

Maponus: I. A. Richmond, *Archaeologia Aeliana*, 4th series, xxi (1943), 206–10.

Cocidius: I. A. Richmond and J. McIntyre, *Archaeologia Aeliana*, 4th series, xiv (1937), 103–9.

Belatucadrus: Transactions of the Cumberland and Westmorland Antiquarian and Archaeological Society, N.S., xxxii, 136–7.

Contrebis: E. Birley, *Cumberland and Westmorland Antiquarian and Archaeological Society's Transactions*, N.S., xlvi (1947), 135–7.

Verbeia: Corpus Inscriptionum Latinarum, vii, 208.

Setlocenia: K. Jackson, *Language and History in Early Britain* (1953), 325.

Vanauns: Transactions of the Cumberland and Westmorland Antiquarian and Archaeological Society, N.S., xxii, 209.

Oceanus: Northumberland County History, xiii, 512–13, 543–5.

Earith statue: Victoria County History, Huntingdonshire, i (1926), 264.

Ranksborough Jupiter: British Museum Guide to the Antiquities of Roman Britain (1951) pl. xvi.

Nero: British Museum Guide to the Antiquities of Roman Britain (1951), pl. xiv.

Capheaton paterae: British Museum Guide to the Antiquities of Roman
    Britain (1922), 90–3.

Backworth hoard: British Museum Guide to the Antiquities of Roman Britain
    (1922), 62–3.

Mithras: London, Journal of Roman Studies, ii, 143 (older discovery);
    R. L. S. Bruce-Mitford, *Recent Archaeological Excavations in Britain*
    (London, 1956), 139–42.

Lullingstone: Archaeologia Cantiana, lxiii (1951), 1–49.

F. Haverfield, 'Early British Christianity', *English Historical Review*,
    xi (1896), 417–30.

R. P. Wright, *Catalogue of the Roman inscribed and sculptured stones in the
    Grosvenor Museum, Chester* (Chester, 1955), 13–15.

Victory: Journal of Roman Studies, xvi (1926), 9–11.

Feriale Duranum: Yale Classical Studies, vii (1940), 1–222.

Disciplina: I. A. Richmond, Archaeologia Aeliana, 4th series, xxi (1943),
    165–9.

Maryport altars: L. P. Wenham, Transactions of the Cumberland and
    Westmorland Antiquarian and Archaeological Society, N.S., xxxix
    (1939), 19–30.

Armilustrium: Yale Classical Studies, vii (1940), 163, 287.

Clarian Apollo: Germania, xxiii (1939), 189–90.

E. Birley, 'Marcus Cocceius Firmus, an epigraphic study', *Proceedings
    of the Society of Antiquaries of Scotland*, lxx (1935–6), 363–77.

Minerva: Archaeologia Aeliana, 4th series, xxi, 154–5.

Ollototae: F. Haverfield, Archaeologia Aeliana, 2nd series, xv (1892),
    225–7.

Anextlomarus: Archaeological Journal, xlv, 171.

Thincsus: Archaeologia Aeliana, 2nd series, x, 148–72; Archaeologia
    Aeliana, 3rd series, xix (1922), 185–97.

Garmangabis: Archaeologia Aeliana, 2nd series, xvi, 313–27.

Unseni Fersomari: Transactions of the Cumberland and Westmorland
    Antiquarian and Archaeological Society, N.S., xi, 470–2.

F. Haverfield, 'Early Northumbrian Christianity and the altars to the
    Di Veteres', *Archaeologia Aeliana*, 3rd series, xv, 22–43.

Dolichenus: Archaeologia Aeliana, 4th series, xxi (1943), 179–93.

R. C. Bosanquet, 'Excavations at Housesteads; the temple of Mithras',
    Archaeologia Aeliana, 2nd series, xxv (1904), 255–63.

I. A. Richmond, J. P. Gillam, and E. Birley, 'The Temple of Mithras
    at Carrawburgh', *Archaeologia Aeliana*, 4th series, xxix (1951),
    1–92.

J. P. Gillam and I. MacIvor, 'The Temple of Mithras at Rudchester',
    ibid., xxxii (1954), 176–219.

INDEX